LOVE HEALS BABY ELEPHANTS
REBIRTHING IVORY ORPHANS

MARY BAURES

Copyright © 2015 by Mary Baures
Library of Congress Control Number 2015952934
ISBN 978-1-939166-85-2

All rights reserved. No part of this book may be reproduced or transmitted in any form or by any means, electronic or mechanical, including photocopying, recording, or by any information storage and retrieval system, without permissions in writing from the copyright owner.

This book was published by Merrimack Media
Cambridge, Massachusetts, 2015

For Mbegu, Kamok, Naipoki, Loijuk, my elephant babies, who came back from devastation with a song in their step, love in their hearts, and joy in their wiggly trunks.

And for my colleagues at the Boston Global March for Elephants and Rhinos, Andrea Zeren, Elise Noelle-Lailiberte, Amy Shroff, Cindy Katsapetses, Gail Sullivan, David Seldon, Glenna Waterman, Lisa and Linda Lewicki and the wise stewardship of Rosemary Alles.

INTRODUCTION

This book is a celebration of healing set against a backdrop of suffering. Watching the life-force bloom in these tiny calves after seeing their families mutilated for ivory is magical.

When everything they loved was lost, they contracted in cornered horror. Sometimes they were so emaciated when rescued that their temperatures plummeted. The other orphans wrapped their trunks around newcomers and caressed them with the heart-shaped ends. Many elephant hearts created a melody to which the newcomers' bodies harmonized. Sparkle came back in their eyes, warmth gushed into their blood, and they fought to live. Gradually, in a womb of surrogate mothering, they bloomed with the juice of spring.

Seeing these toddlers recover and learn to love again, I glimpsed a hidden harmony in the universe and felt a kinship to the vast, miraculous force from which we came.

As an African wildlife photographer, I have been knocked breathless by wild elephants. In water, they make rainbows as they squirt each other and frolic with joy. Up close, they are a wrinkly violet and lift their trunks in a salute. At sunset, their huge, gray shapes glow pink. They dust themselves orange and turn purple at night. Despite their ungainly bulk, they tread delicately beside their babies, stroking them with their trunks.

Helpless without their mothers, calves totter along with poor eyesight and coordination. Sometimes they trip on their bobbing, elastic nose, then suck it like a thumb. Sometimes the mother's trunk lifts like a periscope to scan for danger. For elephants, there is no safety.
We travel in Land Rovers and cut our engines when they pause to listen. The jungle is alive with bird and monkey calls, to signal a leopard stalking nearby. That is not the menace elephants fear. They are no match for the teams of poachers, trophy hunters, and corrupt governments who have waged war on them.

Africa is a fierce landscape made fiercer by human technology. Criminal gangs with helicopters, assault rifles, and rocket-propelled grenades target herds of females with babies, because several can be slaughtered at once. Many are butchered in every raid. The carnage is constant and ongoing.

To hack another creature to death, especially one as loving, peaceful, and wise as a mother elephant, must shrivel one's heart to a raisin. One must hold part of one's mind distant and jab with a shard of one's brokenness. Some delusion of superiority must deny kinship with other beings of the Earth.

African landscapes are littered with the bones of the fallen. All that's left of an elephant are jawbones, chewing nothing but sand. Gone is the trunk caressing her baby. Gone are the grin and the pleasure.

The ivory wars are a symbol of the worse in human nature. This book is about people who represent the best. Their love heals a few lucky massacre survivors—the babies. Without their families, calves have no protection from hyenas and lions and starve without their mother's milk.

Some of the local ranchers and tribes, upon seeing a stranded elephant baby, alert the David Sheldrick Wildlife Trust, which sends a plane to rescue the calf. Only a scant few survive. "For every baby rescued," says the organization's founder, Daphne Sheldrick, "hundreds didn't make it." Given their fragility and innocence, their survival is miraculous.

There is hope for elephants. The murder of Cecil the lion by a dentist was a tipping point—that magic moment when anger over animal cruelty gained momentum and became an outrage tsunami. Cecil is every baby elephant who has nightmares of his mother's face cut off.

The world cares. I hope we save our tender gardeners of the earth. A world without elephants is one of crushed flowers, dead rainbows, and broken trumpets.

TABLE OF CONTENTS

1. LOVE HEALS BABY ELEPHANTS..................................1
2. PEOPLE ADOPT THEM..5
2. LOVE AND HEALING..19
3. THE VALUE OF PLAY...23
4. THE WILL TO LIVE..33
5. GRADUATION FROM THE NURSERY...............................41
6. JUST AS BRILLIANT AS BIG..................................55
7. PSYCHOLOGICAL EXTINCTION..................................61
8. THE ELEPHANT HOLOCAUST....................................65
9. THE TRUE ORPHANS..69
10. MOTHER EARTH...81
11. STIRRINGS OF HOPE..93
12. MURDER OF CECIL...103
13. CONSCIOUSNESS CHANGE....................................107
14. HOW TO MAKE A DIFFERENCE................................111

All photographs by Mary Baures

MARY BAURES

As a psychologist, Mary Baures specializes in helping people recover from horrific loss. She is an African wildlife photographer who adopted four traumatized baby elephants who watched their families massacred for ivory. This book explores their miraculous journey back to trust and love.

Dr. Baures is the author of *Undaunted Spirits – Portraits of Recovery from Trauma*, and many other publications on healing. She is co-producer of the documentary film, *Strong at the Broken Places - Turning Trauma Into Recovery*.

She holds a doctorate in clinical psychology from Antioch New England and a Certificate of Advanced Graduate Study in Human Development from Harvard University. She and her therapy dog, Garth, have a private practice in Beverly, Massachusetts. She is one of the organizers of the Boston Global March for Elephants and Rhinos.

MARY BAURES

LOVE HEALS BABY ELEPHANTS; REBIRTHING IVORY ORPHANS

Orphaned baby elephants scurry back from the field. Wobbly trunks guide pudgy shapes with flapping ears. Orange, red, and green blankets shield their skin from the sun, because babies in the wild move in their mothers' shade. Caretakers in green coats and white safari hats trot with them.

When the orphans see a line of keepers holding bottles of milk, dust explodes at their feet. They break into a gallop toward the keepers, where they wiggle in anticipation of the bottle. As they suck, they stare with rapt attention at their new human family. Here, at the David Sheldrick Wildlife Trust in Nairobi, human love is healing human cruelty, although nothing will take away the memories of what made this orphanage necessary.

Calves hear their families screaming in pain, then watch them mutilated for their ivory. After their mother never emerges from her body, they begin a harrowing ordeal. Terrified, they wander around alone and confused. Without their mothers' milk they can only survive three weeks. Every night threatens to set lions afoot.

Who they were was part of a family, leaning against or touching their mothers most of the time. Their mother was helped by nannies - aunts, sisters, and cousins - who followed, fondled, and

LOVE HEALS BABY ELEPHANTS

fussed over them and responded to their squeaky cries for help. Their eyesight is poor and some fall down wells. Those who try to join other herds are not embraced. Sometimes they wiggle tiny trunks into car windows looking for help, but they
never know when people will become monsters.

In addition to the armed gangs in helicopters, local tribesmen seeking to trade ivory for cash, attack them with guns, poisoned arrows and spears. Two calves, Barsilinga and Zongoloni, were found bravely protecting dying mothers who had been shot. Zongoloni comforted her mother with her trunk. Refusing to leave, she drank urine to survive.

Fear of humans saved the life of Rorogi. Still milk-dependent, he miraculously survived for a month on his own. He was near the village of the Duruma tribe, who have a taste for elephant
meat. Luckily, he found refuge on a farm with dense thickets to hide in, vegetation to eat, and water.

Secretive and quiet, he evaded notice by farm workers. The owner caught a glimpse of him and called anti-poaching rangers. Skilled at hiding, he vanished into dappled shadows for 24 hours before rangers caught him. His avoidance of people hints at the human savagery he must have witnessed when he lost his family.

Other tragedies are from human-wildlife conflict. On May 15, 2014, the Kenyan Wildlife Service shot an elephant who killed a woman. The entire herd stampeded, leaving tiny Mbegu behind. The Kimanjo community speared her in revenge. The injured calf sought refuge in a school but was stoned by the children. The warden of the nearby Naibunga Conservancy rescued Mbegu and secured her in a classroom, while his personnel calmed the agitated community baying for her blood. Traumatized and bleeding from several spear wounds, Mbegu crumpled against a wall. Soon keepers from the orphanage arrived to protect her, clean her cuts, and give her milk. Thankfully, all of her wounds healed without infection.

Ishaq B miraculously survived for a month without her mother, because she befriended a baboon troop, who dropped mangoes on the ground for her. When she was finally rescued, her wounded knee was treated by the orphanage veterinarian. Then she was wrapped in a purple blanket, and the other orphans were brought to welcome her. As their little trunks caressed her, she sensed the other babies were not afraid of their keeper and allowed him to kiss her forehead.

As a clinical psychologist who specializes in trauma recovery, I have adopted four traumatized baby elephants. Since I adopted my first baby elephant in 2006, there has been a dramatic increase in poaching. Elephant populations are in free-fall. The ten million elephants of a century ago have dropped to less than 300,000, all precious remnants of a dying race. Every year, more than 15 percent are butchered. An estimated 35,000 elephants were killed last year.

To quote Edmund Burke, "The only thing necessary for the triumph of evil, is for good men to do nothing." Good people are fighting back, but will it be enough to save this majestic species? Curbing the demand for ivory is the key to halting the killing, but it is a monumental task. Meanwhile, people are doing what they can to help the most helpless victims of the ivory wars.

PEOPLE ADOPT THEM

Powerful tools of social media have enabled their stories to go viral. The cruelty inflicted on them wrings compassion from people around the world who donate to save them. Through monthly photos and news, foster parents witness a marvelous transformation. Withdrawn into a dark world without their mothers, grieving calves are like a tight bud. Gradually, tenderness nudges open terror's grip. A poem, "The Bud" by Galway Kinnell, describes this process: "Sometimes it is necessary to reteach a thing its loveliness – to put a hand on the brow of the flower and retell it in words and in touch it is lovely until it flowers again from within at self-blessing." Opening to love, they bloom with surefootedness and joy.

As they recover, photos of little wrinkled calves tottering around in bright coats with ears fluttering are a gift of grace. A calf does not know what to do with his wiggly trunk, which has 100,000 muscles. When not using it to reach, touch, or smell, he tosses it up and down, whacks himself with it, or sucks it like a thumb. Their faces are both sweet and comical.

Elephants are kindred spirits. Like humans, they have long lifespans, similar developmental stages, and complex neurobiology. They have empathy and come to the aid of others in distress.

Foster parents watch their calves develop distinctive personalities. After all the savagery done to them, calves meet the world with good hearts. The orphans are not doomed to succumb to the vicious things done to them. They can manage, endure, and triumph.

> **Far away from the glittering Chinese shops where elephants are turned into trinkets, their babies recover in a sanctuary.**

Nestled in acacias and Ipomoea creepers with delicate white flowers, their new home is a magical place with a deep reverence for life. Magpies, starlings, and crickets twitter marching music to men in green coats pushing wheelbarrows piled high with giant bottles of milk. A warthog patched up after a lion attack and her four piglets trot behind them. The warthog, the men's shoes, and the bushes at the edge of the paths are fringed with yellow dust, like pollen, an Indian symbol of rebirth.

On both sides of the trail, orphans are chewing leaves, drinking water, or nuzzling each other through the slats of their stalls. The elephant holocaust filled the orphanage to capacity in 2013. To hold 44 residents, more stables had to be built. Older, stabilized calves were sent to one of the rehabilitation facilities. Vurea, who almost died of milk deprivation, is bellowing for another bottle. At a public viewing, he tried to trick the keepers into giving him another jug by washing the milk from his mouth and standing in line again.

Playful Kithaka notices visitors so he rests his trunk on the top of a stable door, climbs up, waggles both legs out, then twirls his trunk like a propeller. His eyes twinkle when his audience laughs and comes over to visit. When he is out of his stall, he enjoys targeting cameramen with mischievous pranks. Earlier in the day a huge python unfurled himself at Kithaka. He screamed, bolted, and caused a stampede. He was brought to the sanctuary because he was separated from his mother when villagers chased away his family.

In another stall, an older resident rolls up her trunk, tips her head up, and squirts water way back in her mouth. Then she limps to a tree limb. Twisting a branch with vegetation to one side, she reaches for more as she chews. She awaits transfer to the new facility in the Kibwezi Forest for those with disabling poaching wounds.

Maxwell the Rhino

A warthog and two piglets have snuck into Maxwell's stall and stolen his sugarcane treats. Maxwell is a blind rhino whose skin is like a prehistoric suit of armor. Using sound and vibrations, he has homed in on one of the tiny thieves who oinks frantically as he escapes under the fence.

Maxwell is in love with Solio, a female who used to be in the pen next to his but is now free and part of the Black rhino community. In 2010, she was found at six months old, standing over her mother, who had a shattered shoulder. Her mother's injury kept her from protecting Solio. When first captured, Solio's agitation was soothed with a tickling brush.

When Maxwell gallops in circles with his tail erect, Solio is coming. After her visit, he escaped following her scent, but keepers lured him back with a wheelbarrow of his dung so he could smell the way home. Vets have tried to restore his sight but were not successful, so he will be a permanent resident. Rhinos in captivity live up to 40 years old.

Rhinos are much more social than at first thought. Lawrence Anthony, in *The Last Rhinos,* describes how Heidi, an orphan adopted by a herd of wildebeest, played sentinel duty and mimicked the wildebeest bulls' warning calls. Heidi imitating her pals. Wildebeests befriending a lonely rhino orphan is part of the amazing connection between all creatures.

The word rhinoceros means "horned-nose." The horn grows five weeks after birth and is prized by the Vietnamese as a virility enhancer. A rumor swept Vietnam that a politician's cancer was cured by rhino horn, made from keratin, the same substance as fingernails. Huijun Shen, president of the UK Association of Traditional Chinese Medicine, said there is no record of using horn to treat cancer in two millennia of Chinese medical texts. It has the pharmacological effects of chewing one's fingernails. But small wits and limp penises are causing these magnificent animals to be slaughtered every six hours, and the pace is accelerating. All five rhino species are threatened with extinction, but Black rhinos are teetering on the brink.

White rhinos are actually gray with a squared, wide lip used for grass grazing. The Dutch named them "wide-mouth," but the English believed they were saying "white." They have a distinct hump above their shoulders and are bigger with smaller skulls than Black rhinos. Calves are nurtured for three years.

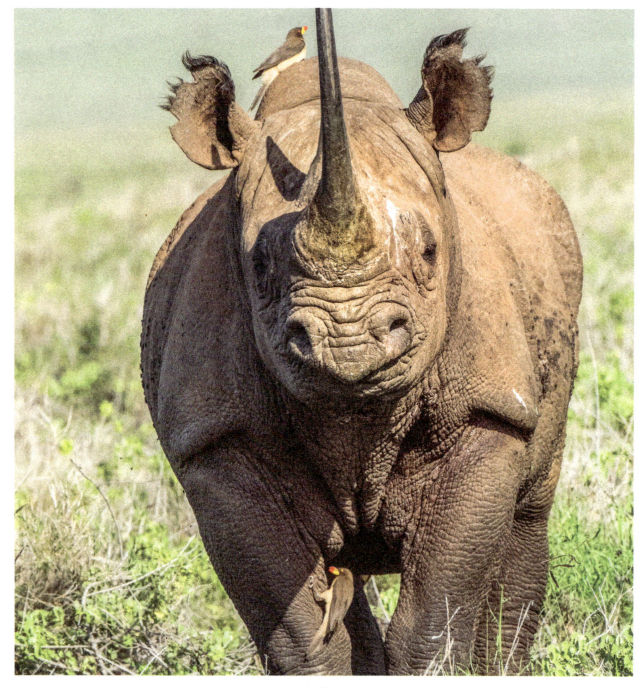

Black rhinos have a pointed upper lip for feeding on bushes, fruit and leaves.

Ox-peckers, colorful birds, have a symbiotic relationship with rhinos. They eat ticks and bugs and create a commotion whenever danger is coming.

Ten orphaned calves have been reared in the Sheldrick nursery. Rhinos are fiercely territorial. They do not accept newcomers into their crash, as a group of rhinos is called. Every day, a keeper takes the orphans to visit rhino dung piles and urinals in their area to deposit dung. After three years, their stall door is left open all night, so the calves can mingle with wild herds and become part of the social structure.

In 1991, after the Maasai speared her mother, Scud, her female calf, was rescued by Richard Leakey, director of the Kenyan Wildlife Service at the time. For days, she defended her mother's decaying body and was mauled by hyenas and lost her tail. With keepers to feed her, she matured and was released into the wild until she got pregnant and damaged her leg. She managed to hop on three legs back to keepers, who nursed her until her delivery of a son, Magnum, in 1997. Magnum became part of the local rhino community and, like Solio, visits the orphanage regularly.

Qumquat's Daughter

On October 30, 2012, a new orphan arrived. Her mother, Qumquat, was one of Amboseli's best-loved matriarchs, with long, distinctive, crossed tusks.

Qumquat led her family to water during droughts, showed them what to eat, what not to eat, and kept them safe for four decades. In 2009, she was treated for gunshot wounds by Dr. David Ndeereh with the Trust's Tsavo Mobile Unit. She survived until 2012, when Tanzania poachers butchered her and her two daughters, Qantina and Quaye.

Quanza, her 10-month-old traumatized calf, stood vigil all night over her mother's carcass. With her trunk, she felt her mother's chest for life, but her mother's coldness horrified her. She remembered the pleasure she felt when her mother looked at her through thick, wiry eyelashes and the loving expression in her face, criss-crossed with tiny wrinkles. Now her mother's face was gone. Moonlight illuminated what poachers did to get every splinter of ivory. She barely knew who she was without her mother, who was like the Earth from which she came.

A blanket covered her face during the ride to the orphanage. The men holding her smelled like men who shot her family. It was dark when she arrived in a stall with a straw floor. The cloth was removed, but horror had turned the world into fragments.

Everything was strange as she tried to absorb the loss of her mother, a pain like an opened wound. The men offered milk in a giant white jug with a nipple. It didn't smell at all like mama. Where was mama? Would these men hurt her too? Her eyes opened wide, and she trumpeted. She tried to flee, but her shoulder hit wooden walls.

Moonlight slanted into her stall between planks of pine. Then a man carried a brighter light in his hand. Discs of light skidded around as he got close and poured drops of milk in her mouth. She was so thirsty, she wanted more, but she was panicking to get away from the menace of the men. The whole night was a frightened blur. Terrible memories of the earth trembling, explosions, clouds of dust, gave her panic and terror. The stark love in her mother's face was mixed with the terrible sounds she made when hurt. She lifted her trunk toward the great arc of stars, hoping to catch a whiff of her mother. The memory of her mother's coldness sunk into her.

Mud baths protect their skin from the African sun. Whooshing into a pile-up helps develop friendships.

The family baby, her playmate, had shrieked during the explosions and fled. He was too helpless and young to be alone. She lifted her trunk to catch his scent, but smelled other elephants, not him. Along with her family, he was lost. The stable seemed like it was closing in. She sucked in gulps of air.

She didn't understand the men's words, an incantation repeated over and over, but their voices were soft and gentle. The light they carried gave their faces a yellowish cast. She backed away, not sure she was safe.

In the morning, she saw the stables set in brown and green of croton trees. Other empty stalls awaited the straggling procession of calves with bobbing heads returning from the fields. They raced toward milk bottles, sucked greedily, then wrapped their little trunks around the keepers' necks and squealed with delight at tender touch and playful voices. The keepers' smiles were full of warmth and white teeth. They were not like the killers whose mouths snarled and growled.

The orphans noticed the new arrival. They sensed a withdrawing that drew them near. They reached their tiny trunks into Quanza's stall. The ends of their trunks were shaped like upside-down hearts. Many baby elephant hearts caressed her. They rumbled a greeting. The frightened newcomer relaxed a little. The connection soothed her.

Quanza was paired with a gregarious calf to introduce her around. Each day her comfort increased and her terror receded. Some tenacity and desire to survive captured her. She came alive in the dance of sharing. She made friends with Ishaq B, who had been saved by baboons and Rorogoi who had hidden in a farm. However, she felt her mother in dreams, which became nightmares. She woke screaming at the buzzing of the electric saw that had cut off her mother's face. But in the morning her eyes were soft again. Tragedy had not made them hard.

How she found joy and possibility is a mystery. In February 2014, the Trust posted photos of Quanza with friends. With a floppy head waggle, she sat on her haunches and invited others to play. They wiggled against her in a spectacular mud wallowing. Slithering around, splashing, sliding up and down, Quanza, for the moment, was happy.

"Elephants are like people," says Keeper Mishak Nzimbi, who places his crumpled safari hat on one of the orphans.

"If you love them, they will love you too."

LOVE AND HEALING

This is Kamok

Accepting affection from others blooms into tenderness, friendship, and love offered to others. Joyful interactions spur brain growth and lay the foundation for future relationships, vital to survival. The brain grows the most rapidly during the first three or four years, and relationships help wire it.

Trauma damages the calf's ability to process what is happening and regulate emotions, but love pulls them into the world where skills are learned. Soothing touch fosters the ability to feel close and releases growth hormones.

The orphans develop resilience in a womb of surrogate mothering. Gradually they reweave a social fabric with other orphans to mimic the one they lost. The older females focus on one of the babies for special nurturing. Sonje, the nursery matriarch, leaves her group at noon and visits the babies, who squeal with delight. She caresses them with her trunk. Then she lies down so they climb over her for cuddles.

A new family of human caretakers replaces abandonment with belonging. The cries of pain from their massacred families are replaced by playful voices calling their names. All night the youngsters are caressed, sung to, and fed. In the daytime, their muscles are strengthened with soccer, mud baths, and trips to the forest. Terror is soothed and new abilities awakened. Eventually, they trust again.

Kamok

Nursery babies are fed under a hanging blanket steeped in elephant aroma. Resting their tiny trunks on it brings back a safe time when their mothers were alive. They all want to be closer to the surrogate wool mama. Ashaka swats the others with her wet noodle trunk and then shoulders them. Kauro pushes back. Kamok steps between them to make peace. She has emerged as the matriarch of the baby set. When older calves visit to mother the babies, Kamok leads them back to the keepers. She does not want to share the leadership role.

On September 8, 2013, Kamok tottered into the Ol Pejeta Conservancy on unstable legs. Abandoned by her family just after birth, she may not have fed from her mother even once. When rescued, her ears were petal pink and she was covered in soft fuzz. Her umbilical cord was fresh, and the pads of her feet were hardly used. Because Kamok may not have received her mother's natural antibodies, the keepers transfused plasma from an adult elephant into her small body while she slept on a mattress. Because her joints were weaker than they should have been, she couldn't keep up with her family. But in the safety of the stockade, her legs grew stronger.

In the rescue footage, Kamok totters. Wobbly joints tip her over. She tries to get up but trips on her bobbing elastic trunk. One imagines the terror she must have felt after being abandoned for not being able to keep up. A matriarch will not risk the others' lives. It is tragic her mother, who can only bear an infant every two years, had to leave her.

I adopted Kamok in 2014. She follows her new human family trustingly, because she never saw her mother mutilated by people. Her eyes sparkle as her keeper caresses her. Her rough start in life has not damaged her beyond repair. Her head shows halos of fuzz in the sunlight as she trumpets squeakily and flaps her ears, then charges a warthog, not much smaller than she is. Her mischievousness is encouraged by her best friend, Ashaka, who joins in the fun. But they halt when the warthog stands her ground.

When the public visits, Kamok trots down the visitor's cordon, bumping into the school children who scream and laugh, delighting baby Kamok. She is gaining control of her trunk and caresses others with it when they head to the mud bath. But without her mother, who became tense when there was danger, it is hard for her to know when she's safe. When buffalos appear, she darts into the brush. On one occasion, she was only found two hours later.

In her stable, dust particles climb up and down ladders of light as night sets in. Her keeper cuddles her, sings to her, and sleeps with her. Every three hours a small trunk reaches out and tugs his blanket. It's time for another bottle of milk. "If you leave her alone she will cry," her keeper says.

When Yao Ming, a 7 foot, 6 inch Chinese NBA star, visited the Trust, he met Kamok wrapped in a red plaid blanket. Her step bounced and her eyes brightened as she reached her trunk to him. Her joy impressed him so much, he said she would beat the odds and survive.

He knew how fragile calves are because a male calf had pushed against him for comfort. Photos of the him with the two-week old Kinango went viral because his 7ft. 6 inch frame towered over the tiny elephant. Soon afterward, however, Kinango died.

The health of the orphans is fragile and can deteriorate rapidly. On April 17, 2015, one of the nursery babies, Ashaka, became too weak to stand, refused to eat or drink, and died. When she first arrived in November 2013, she was three weeks old and had been trapped in a drying water hole. Her condition was monitored because staff knew a water victim would have a tough time with teething. To their surprise, all eight teeth burst through. She recovered with boundless energy. She loved to wiggle her trunk around a bottle when drinking. Her surprising death shocked and saddened the staff and especially Kamok, who looked everywhere for her. They were both daunted by the size of the older orphans and stuck near each other during their first fragile days.

Mbegu was moved to the stall next to Kamok, so they could comfort each other in their grief. Mbegu, the calf attacked by villagers, first calmed her terror by contact with Ashaka, who also helped her trust people even though humans had done savage things to her.

Ndotto became another companion for Kamok and Mbegu. He was discovered confused among sheep and goats by the nomadic Samburu tribe who were shocked to have a baby elephant among their livestock. Just after giving birth, humans frightened Ndotto's mother. Ndotto was found as a newborn with a fresh umbilical cord, fuzz on his head, pink ears, and very long eyelashes. Innocently, he followed the herdsmen, thinking they were his family. They contacted the Trust.

Because the orphans are so fragile, it is necessary for them to be part of a family. Too much dependence on just one other elephant could trigger the loss of their mother if their companion suddenly dies, as Ashaka did.

The youngest calves, Kamok, Ashaka, Kauro, and Mbegu consoled Mwashoti. With a foot the size of a basketball, he was unable to browse with the older orphans. The nursery babies provided companionship, slowed down for him, and were extremely gentle as they foraged together.

On Valentine's Day of 2015, Mwashoti was seen with a huge wound from a cable snare cutting through a joint in his leg. His mother accompanied him, but she had to leave the herd because he could barely walk. In March, his leg became infected and needed aggressive treatment, so both were anesthetized. Mwashoti could not have healed in the wild. He was brought to the orphanage where vets packed his leg in green clay and gave him heavy doses of antibiotics. At first, his survival seemed impossible, but the company of nursery babies and a strong will to live contributed of what staff see as a miracle healing.

On June 23, 2015, another calf was brought from the Rumuruti Forest with a snare like Mwashoti's. Even more horrendously, a spear had pierced his forehead but not his feisty spirit. The tragic little figure, Simotua, fought fiercely to live. His wounds confined him to his stockade, but he seemed forlorn when the other babies left for the bush. Finally, on July 9, the giant hole in his head green from protective clay, he joined Mwashoti and the others, who surrounded him with elephantine comfort and joy. Playfully, he swung his trunk and charged ostriches Pea and Pod, who scampered away.

MARY BAURES

THE VALUE OF PLAY

These two orphans take time out of their soccer game to toss dirt over their heads.

When immobilized by terror, all strong emotions upset their fragile equilibrium, so when calves play exuberantly, they are no longer grievously distressed. In playful abandon, they show life is joyful again.

Mud baths are an important part of the noon public viewing. They crouch on haunches, then flop into mud. They whoosh, writhe, and wiggle against each other and toboggan into a pile-up. They use their trunks to fling mud onto themselves, making a slapping sound as they turn from iridescent gray-purple to orange. Teleki climbed on top of Orwa, who tipped him off and sat on him. The laughter of the crowd encouraged them, so they repeated the sparring several more times.

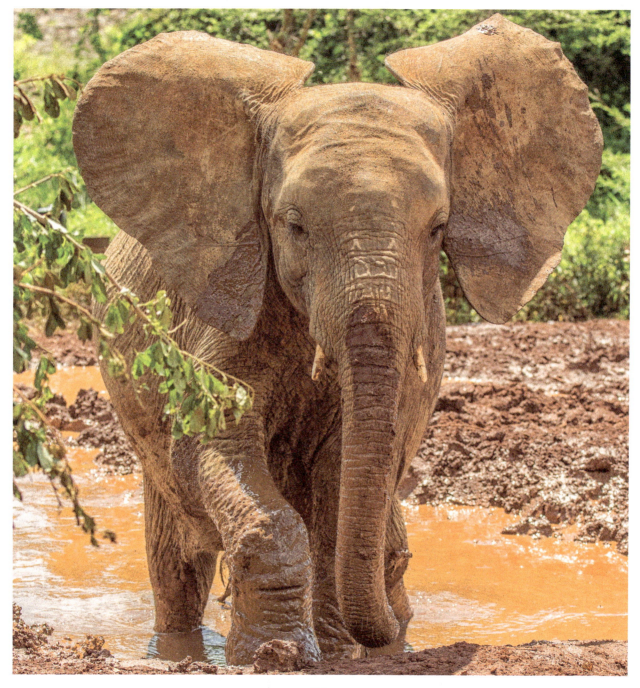

Pea and Pod.

Sometimes Mbegu shows off to the crowd, spraying mud toward them. Then she makes a dramatic display by emerging out of the mud and sliding back down. When she dusts herself, she poses with her head held high and her trunk spinning like a propeller, round and round. The audience usually claps, which eggs her on.

Kamok sometimes plays with Maxwell the blind rhino. She fondles his ears, which he loves. One time she got Mbegu and Mwashoti to join her, but Mwashoti likes wrestling and tried to pull Maxwell's horn through the gate. Mbegu, always protective of others, tried to stop him and they started a pushing game. Meanwhile, Maxwell, in the spirit of fun, butted the gate with his horn in bluff combat, and then ran in circles and jumped up and down.

Other kinds of play include soccer, slinging dirt in the air, and tag. Play helps young calves read social cues and hone motor skills. It is a complex dance with split-second communications and assessments of each other's abilities. The slightest turn of a head or wave of a trunk has meaning.

They seem comical because their heads are big in proportion to their bodies. With a loose, floppy gait, they shake from side to side, rippling ears like canvas sails. Trunks waggling, froth flowing from their mouths, the pursuer grabs the tail of the squealing fleer. Their joy is pure.

Males butt heads, trunk-wrestle, spare and joust. Like sumo wrestlers, they totter back and forth shoving each other. In mock combat, they compete for dominance.

Spontaneous play is contagious. They race feathered friends, two ostriches, Pea and Pod, who also arrived as orphans. Although the ostriches only have two legs, they always win. They can run 70 kilometers per hour and split up to confuse the elephants who gallop in pursuit. They dart and swerve, causing the elephants to crash into each other. When they are on the ground, the ostriches daintily jump over them and the game begins again.

When Mbegu was browsing at some wild fruit, the two ostriches snatched what she reached for before she got it. She abandoned those branches and chased Pea and Pod away. But they ran back and danced around her in circles. When they laid their necks on the ground, Mbegu trumpeted with flailed ears and charged. They knew she was serious and fled, but they materialized again to tease her when she went back to her fruit.

One of the prime benefits of play is feeling in control. Players are free agents, not agents in someone else's game. In the horrific trauma of seeing their families murdered, they were helpless. In recovery, they learn their actions matter and can bring positive results. They can act out aggression in socially acceptable ways and revise images of themselves and the world. In self-exploration and expansion, they are glad about who they are and that they are alive. Such vitality shows they are no longer overwhelmed by fear.

ANIMALS LEARN BY PLAYING

Play is pleasurable, helps animals make friends, and develops problem-solving skills. In self-directed fun, they express their individuality and release energy. In 1963, Mason, Sharpe, and Saxon conducted a study on the play of young chimpanzees. They found social play to be more favored than unfavored food and as equally desired as fruit, their favorite food.

Play can override hunger. Nobert Rosing was out in the deep snow in northern Canada with Eskimo sled dogs when a polar bear appeared. The bear seemed to be zeroing in on one of the dogs, Hudson. Rosing figured it was all over for Hudson. She crouched down in a play bow, then wagged her tail. The mood changed into a ballet. The bear nuzzled the dog. The dog licked the bear. The dog rolled onto her back. The bear rolled with her. They tumbled, hugging and licking. Play signals cross species, but only when they feel safe.

In 2003, in Juneau, Alaska, a wild, black wolf loped toward a Labrador Retriever who got lose from her owner, Nick Jans. The wolf was twice the size of the dog, so Jans was scared when the animals went nose to nose. The wolf bounced and bowed on his forelegs, a play signal. Then he leaned close and lifted a paw. Finally, Dakotah, the dog, responded to calls and retuned to Jans. As if pained by the rejection, the wolf raised his muzzle with an anguished howl.

But this began a six year relationship of play dates between the two. The wolf, who must have been lonely without a pack, had toys stashed away for their encounters.

In Botswana, I photographed two tired and thin mother lions. Parading behind them were nine cubs, whose eyes and ears intently followed the adults. The cubs' playful tumbling, swatting, and chasing were gone. Lions survive on one-quarter of their former ranges and their numbers have declined by 50 percent in 30 years. Fearful, exhausted, and stressed animals spend all their resources on survival.

THE WILL TO LIVE

The strength of the life-force in them is a crucial factor in survival.

Their deepest feelings about life and their place in it influences their will to live. Some newborns who lose their mothers cannot invest in what seems a savage world. A keeper explains, "If a calf has seen his mother killed by people, he believes we are going to kill him so we have to get him quickly to the other elephants."

Their deepest assumptions about the world are shattered. Memories of their mothers being butchered withdraw them into frozen watchfulness. The abrupt disintegration of everything familiar throws them into shock. A primitive instinctual part of the brain takes over. "Playing possum" or freezing is a survival strategy that kicks in when an animal feels trapped and cannot flee or fight. Being inert does not evoke aggression from predators.

Intense fear creates a cascade of biochemical and neuronal responses. If they are fighting dehydration or infection, it's a critical time. Many cannot muster the energy for survival because their spirits have withered.

After the immobilization phase, they have to move beyond collapse. They have to marshal resources for self-preservation. The grotesqueness of the massacre of their family continues to intrude. The sudden disruption of logic about how the world works makes action terrifying. They know viscerally through their connectedness. Without that connectedness, they do not know.

It is crucial they feel their actions matter and can influence their environment. Martin Seligmen conducted a study on learned helplessness on dogs. At first, the dogs could jump to avoid being shocked. When they could no longer avoid the shocks, they just gave up.

Three-month-old Ndume's bellowing for his mother was so frantic, keepers let him out of his stable to search for his mother, speared by farmers after the family wandered into a maize field. Ndume, unconscious from a head wound in the attack, had not witnessed his mother's death. Once out of the stable, he tore around in a desperate hunt. After he was sure his mother was not around, a profound grief began. He screamed when asleep, reliving the attack on him in nightmares.

Mbegu

Mbegu, the calf speared by angry villagers, also had trouble sleeping. Babies sleep touching their mothers. Mbegu wound her little trunk toward Ashaka in the next stable. She tried climbing between the bars but wouldn't fit. Finally out of the stable, she gripped Ashaka's trunk and held on for dear life. When Ashaka rolled around in the dirt, Mbegu leaned on her for comfort. Green clay healed the infections from deep wounds in her rump and neck, but healing from the loss of her mother is ongoing. Although she arrived with her teeth already cut, she was the smallest calf keepers had seen. They named her "Mbegu," Swahili for seed. They thought she was tiny because she came from a small seed.

In August of 2015, after she recovered from her terror, Mbegu smelled fear in the next stall where Godo paced and charged to keep the keepers away. Godo must have seen the dark things people do to elephants. Mbegu knew the panic that permeated the air between them. She tried to stroke Godo through the bars, but Godo was too jittery and apprehensive to accept the affection. Mbegu rumbled to calm her. Desperation and suspicion radiated from Godo's cushioned feet to her trunk. Its hairy heart-shaped end raised, moved, and smelled. As Godo's hope of ever seeing her family shriveled, Godo was too agitated and upset to accompany the others. She'd been rescued at six months and vividly remembered her family. She knew they were lost, never to be found.

After a few days when Godo's door was opened, she hid inside. Mbegu tried to soothe her, but

Mbegu with her keeper, Julius Letoiya

Mbegu heals the past by living in the present. She was savagely beaten by humans but has learned to love. Her miraculous survival from several deep spear wounds by angry villagers have not made her hard. There's always softness in her eyes and she protects anyone being bullied.

Godo shoved her aside and burst frantically into the bushes where she charged, raised her ears, and shrieked. The other babies trumpeted back and Godo got more upset and bolted. Mbegu and Kamok followed her and calmed her down. Another time, Mbegu was playing with two of the smaller babies and Godo approached. Mbegu chased her away to protect them from Godo's aggression. Godo's tough act is a more hopeful sign of survival than withdrawal.

Calves need time to heal from their losses before another one comes along. Withdrawn into a dark world between worlds, they carry a heavy emptiness. Loss and isolation elevates glucocorticoid levels, but strong social bonds create a more robust immune system.

No one knows the secret of what wild mothers do when calves are teething from one to four months old. Their babies do not have any problems cutting teeth. At the orphanage, however, teething is life-threatening. Fever, lethargy, and diarrhea are combined with an infection. The entire scenario is worse if they are still deeply grieving. Their damaged spirits sometimes cause their bodies to just shut down.

Although they have horrific memories, some calves latch onto the life-force within them and survive against all odds. How love heals was clear for Loijuk, the first baby I adopted in 2006. She was emaciated when rescued, and her temperature plummeted. Liquid from her lungs seeped out her small trunk. She was turning cold and close to death when the other orphans greeted her. They wrapped their trunks around her. Caresses created a melody to which her body harmonized. Sparkle came into her eyes and she fought to live. She has flourished and now lives entirely self-sufficiently in the wild but comes back to visit the keepers and orphans at the Tsavo Rehabilitation Facility.

Shmetty

The orphanage found out the hard way that orphans shouldn't get too attached to one person. The first baby Daphne Sheldrick saved, Shmetty, stopped feeding when Daphne went away.

Previously, all the milk-dependent babies died because they couldn't digest the fat in cow's milk. When Shmetty, short for the German word for butterfly, was rescued in 1974 she became skeletal with sunken eye sockets and pronounced cheekbones. Daphne mixed coconut oil with baby formula. Magically, it worked. (Later, cooked oatmeal porridge was added.) Shmetty's face grew chubby. Since it looked like she would survive, Daphne's husband made a mud wallow for her. She made friends with ostrich chicks who followed her like a mother. They squatted beside her and didn't seem to mind when she played rough by dragging them around by their necks.

Daphne knew of Shmetty's dependence on her because Shmetty listened for the creak in the gate when Daphne was gone and almost plowed into her on her return. Still, Daphne thought Shmetty would survive because she had grown to almost three feet tall. When Daphne went to her daughter's wedding for two weeks, Shmetty became skeletal, ill, and died. Daphne's absence must have triggered the loss of Shmetty's mother, a trauma so wrenching she died of a broken heart.

"I should have known by watching elephants in the wild," Daphne said. "They are raised by entire families." She meant she should have included some other elephants and caretakers in the relationship. Now calves are cared for by many keepers so they do not become too attached to one person.

Orphans with deep psychic wounds can sometimes heal by teaming up with one special "grieving friend." Their vulnerability is soothed by pressing up against each other and crossing trunks while tears stream down their cheeks. Touch drowns their dread and the comfort of belonging connects them to the life-force still there, underneath shock, grief, and hurt.

"If you are harsh with them," says Keeper Philip Okode, "you will scare them. You have to let them come to you." There are so many heart-breaking stories at the orphanage, it is encouraging for keepers when elephants survive against all odds.

Murera

One such miracle is Murera. When Piers Winkworth, the owner of Offbeat Safaris Camp in Northern Kenya, took guests into the Meru National Park in June of 2012, they saw an elephant in the grass struggling to get up. Severely wounded by a gruesome method of poaching, Murera had stepped on poisoned spikes hidden in the ground. They'd gone through her front foot. Her back leg was swollen and paralyzed and had three deep puncture wounds.

The poison immobilizes the elephant and the blood trail makes the ivory easy to find. Murera,

These two are "grieving friends." They soothe each other's terror and dread by pressing up against one another.

who was two years old, was rescued before the poachers could track her. She was given intravenous life support, and her wounds were cleaned and packed with green clay. The vets considered humanely ending her life because she was in great pain and her prognosis for survival was poor. Murera herself sensed she would never be whole again and slipped into a deep depression.

Opening her stall let her know she was not a prisoner. Another elephant, Orwa, who himself had arrived more dead than alive, was chosen to brighten her mood. Reluctant to lie down because she feared being unable to get up, Murera leaned against railings in her stall. She was unable to put weight on her front foot and the back leg was stiff and badly swollen.

When Orwa was found, he was emaciated. He had been attacked by small predators and had bites all over his body. He was chosen to help Murera because he had recovered from horrific wounds and a deep depression, trailing behind the others, the epitome of misery. Orwa sensed what to do. He took a delicate approach, careful not to unbalance her. Swinging his trunk back and forth toward Murera, she clasped his. Their trunks explored each other, then entwined, and knotted.

Murera brightened and her front foot healed enough for her to put weight on it. Her back leg was still immobile, but the orphanage used homeopathic healing remedies and turmeric for the swelling. A large abscess filled with poison was lanced. She shuffled out to browse in the company of other elephants. Movement came back in her rear leg and soon she was mobile enough for a mud bath.

She stayed at the nursery until June 24, 2014, when the new facility at Umani in the Kibwezi forest, for impaired poaching victims, opened. The vegetation is more plentiful at Umani and does not require as much walking as Tsavo. She was accompanied by Sonje, whose knee was damaged by a bullet.

The severity of the elephants' wounds do not accurately predict who will recover and who will not. Many, like Murera, who had a poor prognosis, survive against all odds. Yet others, with more minor injuries, do not make it.

GRADUATION FROM THE NURSERY

The Voi Rehabilitation Facility/Naipoki

Edwin Lusicki, head keeper at the nursery, says he is happy when babies are strong enough to move on to the next step. After about three years, calves like Naipoki, whom I adopted in 2011, are sent to a rehabilitation facility. After she lost her family, Naipoki fell down a well, and her trunk was mauled by predators. After she recovered from her wounds, developed social skills, and was no longer milk-dependent, she outgrew the nursery.

In addition to Umani, the Trust has two other rehabilitation facilities, at Voi and Ithumba, both in Tsavo National Park. Tsavo is a protected area the size of Michigan. In November of 2013, Naipoki was trucked to the Voi Rehab Center. Disturbing an elephant's social fabric is devastating, so she was sent with her two best girlfriends, Ishaq B and Kihari, who were rescued the same month in 2010. For days before the move, they were coaxed in and out of the elephant-moving truck. Keepers Sammy and Adam accompanied them on the six-hour journey. They were greeted by head keeper Joseph Sauni amid trumpeting, rumbling, and intertwining of trunks with the 19 keeper-dependent juniors, and Emily, the matriarch of the ex-orphans, who are in the wild. Emily was last at Voi in June but knew, through uncanny means, that the juniors were coming.

Mysteriously, ex-orphans anticipate ahead of time the arrival of new nursery elephants," says Sheldrick. "We can only assume telepathy is at work."

Tsavo is hotter than Nairobi, so after greetings, Emily and her calf, Eva, led the newcomers, still red from the nursery dust, to a mud bath. November is the rainy season, so white blooms of wild lilies dotted the lush green backdrop in unremitting sway.

Although keepers accompany them much of the time, elephants at the rehab facilities determine where to browse and come back at night to the safety of the stables. Naipoki followed and was curious to investigate wild herds even when the matriarch was not friendly to her. At the nursery she learned some elephant language, but at Voi she will learn wild social skills and how to survive in the wild.

The language of wild herds has twenty-five sounds and gestures for different concepts. High-frequency sounds include snorts, barks, cries, and trumpets. Some of the subtle discriminations communicate different threat levels, which may be how the orphans tell wild friends that the keepers won't hurt them.

Naipoki will learn low-frequency audio communication and how to listen to sound waves with her limbs. Sometimes wild elephants extend their ears, dig toenails into sand, and swing another foot off the ground to pick up signs of the arrival of other herds.

When Naipoki no longer has caretakers, she'll need to know danger signals. When matriarchs bellow a low, urgent trumpet, lions are coming. She will also learn the other animals' signals. Jackals who see a lion make a sharp staccato bark different from their normal chorus of howls. Lions themselves make soft moans as well as roars. There are greeting and exit rituals at watering holes. When the dominant bull arrives, the other males make room for him at the flow of the freshest water. Once he is in position, the younger bachelors place their trunks in his mouth, like paying respects to a mafia don, before positioning themselves. Sometimes bulls, who are scouts of the elephant world, call repeatedly into the distance before a herd arrives. They seem to be saying, "The coast is clear."

At the rehabilitation facilities, older ex-orphan females have baby-snatching tendencies. There have been aggressive attempts to hijack Naipoki and her two friends. Older ex-orphans pushed them ahead of the column when the newly wild group headed to leave. The keepers thwart their attempts. They are not experienced enough to be in the wild.

In the morning, when Naipoki and her friends are released from their stalls, their day begins with expelling baboons from their dairy cubes. After sparring with the resident impala, they chase the orphaned zebras, who also accompany them at grazing.

As Naipoki makes friends, a few will appear at the stockade to collect her in the evening for a "wild sleepover." The elephant selected for this adventure gets the invitation by "psychic" means and greets the others for the outing. Sometimes scary things happen in the night. When an orphan panics, wild friends escort her back to the stockade. After about eight years of coming and going, Naipoki and a few of her friends will join a wild family. Some of the other 19 orphans at Voi will probably join her when she decides to leave the safety of the stockade. Recently, she entertained a wild bull at mud baths and has become the leader of her girlfriends.

Dusting protects their skin from insects and the harsh sun.

Loijuk - Ithumba

Forty-six ex-orphans have been reared at Ithumba in the northern sector of Tsavo. It holds 38 orphans at one time. In one area, rocks and boulders stretch like a moonscape toward Ithumba Mountain in the distance.

Loijuk, the first baby I adopted, lives here wild. She is part of the group snatching up plants by the roots, as their large gray shapes sluff-sluff along kicking up dust so they become hazy. Loijuk and the others stop to scoop up powdery sand in their trunks and blow it on their heads and backs. She comes with wild and ex-orphan herds to the watering trough, mud baths, and to visit the ten juniors who are still milk- and keeper-dependent. These families will eventually adopt the orphans when they are ready.

When she lived with the other orphans here, Loijuk picked the lock on her night stable twice and escaped. Since orphans decide when they want to become wild, the staff let her go. She'd made friends and had the protection of a wild and ex-orphan herd. She is still part of the orphan social life.

Loijuk is like a big sister who has gone off to college. When she comes home, Teleki tries out pushing tactics with her to use on his fellow junior boys. When a pack of wild dogs headed for the water trough, Loijuk spread her ears and galloped toward them. They took off in a fright. Loijuk also delivered Suguta for treatment of a wound. After Dr. Poghorn made sure it wasn't from a poisoned arrow, Loijuk caressed her through the fence and came back to check on her. Many of the ex-orphans come back when injured.

Protection is reciprocated. When keepers and orphans in the bush are confronted with lions or a grumpy buffalo, the orphans crowd around keepers while the senior orphans chase off the aggressive animals.

For elephants, family is everything. Not all the juniors sent here want to leave their human families. Imenti, who was rescued still in his fetal membrane because he was born while villagers hacked his mother to death, felt most secure with his keepers and was protective of both his human family and orphan family. After a white minivan just missed colliding with his family as they crossed the road, he stood guard at the gate and prevented white minibuses from entering. After complaints, he was sedated and trucked to the Tiva River but took off to find his human family. He searched for them at the Kilaguni Lodge, whose staff alerted his keepers. When they arrived, he happily followed their car to the stockades.

Ndume, found among sheep and goats just after being born, traveled back from Tsavo, where he'd never been before. He'd been sedated and trucked to 100 miles away but traveled back to find his human family.

The crack of an elephant-killing rifle has a sonic boom much like thunder. One night, Simba and a few of his friends got frightened at a thunderstorm and took off. The keepers searched for them unsuccessfully and then had to shut the stockade for the night. Simba got separated from his friends and was attacked by lions. In the morning, he was found in a daze at the scene of a violent battle. Bushes were trampled. His trunk was cut, his ear lobe torn off, and his legs deeply wounded. He must have been successful, though, because he was still standing. Lion hair on the ground was mixed with blood, so the lions must have gone off for an easier meal. His wounds were treated for infections, but he eventually died. His ordeal shows just how vulnerable orphans are without a herd and why leaving the safety of the stockade at night has so many risks.

Most families do not welcome lone elephants. However, loss of their families has taught the orphans compassion for any elephant without a herd. Ex-orphans welcome other elephant "floaters" into their families. Wild recruits, even helpless babies, are usually rejected. In their film *Reflections on Elephants*, Beverly and Derek Joubert, show rare footage of an exceptional case when a baby elephant was accepted. The abandoned baby shrieked into the night for help. Hyenas answered his cry. Just before their attack, they heard elephants approaching and backed off. The matriarch who had her own lactating female calf, greeted the youngster but left him. When she took the family off into the darkness, chilling cries of the abandoned calf followed. The baby's shrill anguish was not easy to resist, so the family returned and gathered the baby up in its forest of legs.

Juniors at the stockades get to know wild families gradually. Because of the water and mud bath the stockade has many wild visitors. At first wild bulls only visited during the night and disappeared in the day but they soon learned that humans were safe. During the dry season, the water is necessary for survival so keepers witness the complex social network of wild herds.

One family who doesn't know another will ignore it. But families who know each other communicate, telling each other when they are coming. They greet each other with trumpeting, tusk clicking, ear flapping, and winding their trunks around each other. Secretions from their temporal glands dribble down along their chins as they vocalize elephantine joy.

Like a parent who has children in a warzone, I fear for my adopted elephants when released in the wild. After watching them survive a harsh beginning, develop skills, and finally trust again, it would break my heart if poachers killed them.

In October 2012, that is what happened to Selengai, a nine-year-old ex-orphan. She was rescued in 2003 and hand-reared since she was one day old. Her slaughter had keepers, staff, and adopted

For elephants, family is everything.

parents weeping. To all who watched her cut teeth, pick things up with a wobbly trunk, and express her floppy-eared joy, her death for two nubs of ivory seemed senseless.

When orphans become wild in Tsavo National Park, they are supposed to be in a safe haven. Selengai joined a group of ex-orphans led by a human-reared matriarch. Poachers killed her with a poison spear lodged deep in her back. Believed to be from the Wakamba tribe neighboring the park, they built a platform from which to spear elephants. When the loving and gentle Selengai browsed nearby, gravity increased the force with which the spear entered her body. She died an agonizing death from the poison while trying to return to the stockades for help.

Staff at the orphanage face tragic deaths the way elephant matriarchs do – by focusing on the living. Selengai had been part of Yatta's ex-orphans herd. Yatta is a natural matriarch who interacts with wild herds and has a deep maternal instinct. Her foot-long tusks are asymmetrical, with the left one pointing higher. At 12 years-old, she mated with a 26 year-old wild bull. Two years later, anticipation was in the air when an excited group, who knew about Yatta's impending labor, were in route to help with the delivery. In January of 2012, she delivered Yetu which in Swahili means "ours."

In January of 2012, when Yatta brought the baby to meet her human family at the Ithumba stockades, a lilac-breasted roller sang and bronze gold grasses swayed. A parade of fifty elephants from all corners of Kenya appeared to celebrate. With roaring and rumbling, huge bodies bustled around the mud bath. Huge feet spreading out like shock absorbers and moved delicately around the precious new arrival. There, only hours old, amid trunk-kisses and tender caresses was Yetu. Protective nannies shaded her from the African sun. Her pink petal ears fluttered as she reached up to suckle, amid cooing and trumpeting. With total trust, Yatta guided her precious baby toward human well-wishers and family. Benjamin Kyalo, the Ithumba head-keeper who helped raise Yatta, stepped forward to caress the baby.

There was harmony between human and elephant families, reflecting the symbiotic love of people and animals so vital to all wildlife.

With total trust, Yatta guided her precious baby toward human well-wishers and family. Benjamin Kyalo, the Ithumba head-keeper who helped raise Yatta, stepped forward to caress the baby.

JUST AS BRILLIANT AS BIG

Elephants are majestic. Their ears, shaped like a map of Africa, are built-in air conditioners. They catch a breeze as blood vessels cool the body. The trunk is versatile, acting as hand, lip, nose, snorkel, hose, and telescopic antenna. Elephants spread seeds, turn woodlands into savannas, clear brush, and make paths. In the dry season when grass is gone, they pull down branches, providing cover and food for smaller creatures. During a drought, they dig for water for other animals. They are vital. Other species would die without them.

Elephants' brains are four times as large as ours. The part of the brain responsible for memory is much more sophisticated than ours. They have remarkable spatial reasoning and transmit low-frequency sounds hundreds of miles. Like parrots, they can imitate what they hear. Mlaika, an orphan whose night shelter was two miles from a road in Tsavo National Park, has copied truck sounds. Calimero, a 23-year-old male elephant in a Swiss zoo, made chirp-like calls to his longtime zoo mates.

Andrea Turkalo of the Elephant Listening Project has compiled an elephant dictionary. When the elephants move away, she assumes it is a warning. If the sound is not followed by a behavior, she doesn't know what it means. After twenty years of study, she has only deciphered a fraction of their vast vocabulary.

In September of 2015, three desperate wild bulls traveled miles to the Ithumba Reintegration Center, because they had been shot by poison arrows. One of them mated and fathered a daughter, Yetu, with an ex-orphan matriarch. The ex-orphans communicated to them that they could receive help from the keepers there. Although humans had tried to kill them, they knew the people at Ithumba were safe. Doctors arrived shortly, who cleaned poison out of their wounds and gave them antibiotics. All three made a complete recovery.

Elephants can distinguish human languages. Studies show that when the Maasai people talk on a loud speaker, elephants run from it. They do not have the same reaction to other languages. Elephants avoid Maasai, with whom they peacefully coexisted until Europeans gave Maasai lands to game reserves. So, in revenge, Maasai speared elephants and rhinos. But they also respect elephants. In their culture, brides who leave their homes are not supposed to look back. According to the fable, when a bride did look back, she became the first elephant. Recently, their standard of living has plummeted, so some are lured by ivory money.

In 2010, Diana Reiss and Preston Foerder tested the problem-solving skills of Kandula, a seven-year-old male, at the National Zoo in Washington, DC. They strung aerial snacks out of reach. Kandula rolled a large plastic cube into a stepstool and stood on it to reach the food. He also used tractor tires and butcher blocks for the same task.

In Amboseli, a researcher went to find a veterinarian and antibiotics because he saw an elephant walking with a spear stuck in her. When they returned, the wounded one had a friend with her, but the spear was gone. They believed it had fallen out. But when the doctor's antibiotic dart hit, they knew what happened. The elephant's friend pulled it out. Elephants sometimes stand on either side of a friend hit by a tranquilizer dart to keep their companion from falling over. Vicki Fishlock, a colleague of elephant researcher Cynthia Moss in Kenya, described chasing a mother away from her baby, who had fallen in a well. It would have been terrifying for the mother to watch her calf roped up, so they drove a truck at the mother and shouted. She turned around and sat on the truck's bumper to stop their advances. She could have charged and done damage, but she had no malice.

Elephants are compassionate and frequently feed other elephants with damaged trunks and come to the aid of people. In Tanganyika, a mother set her baby under a tree. A family of elephants passing by stopped. They pulled down branches and tenderly, without waking the baby, created shade to protect the baby from the sun.

Spooky Action at a Distance

When nursery elephants are sent to Tsavo, the ex-orphans, who are living wild, anticipate when they are coming. They start traveling back to the stockade to greet them with a great outpouring of love. Some new babies are not known by older ones living wild, so the telepathy may be between the ex-orphans and the Nairobi keepers.

Elephants exhibit psychic abilities most of us don't have. When Lawrence Anthony, the elephant whisperer, died in March 2012, thirty-one elephants from two herds arrived after traveling 112 miles. They marched in a solemn line for hours to pay their respects. He saved their lives after they broke out of enclosures and were considered rogue, destined to be shot. They were led by Nana, the matriarch, and had not been to his reserve at Thula Thula for a year and a half. They continued their grief vigil for two days before heading back to the bush. Their knowledge of his passing speaks of the mystical knowing of elephants.

Lawrence Anthony was well aware of their telepathy. Whenever he arrived home from a long trip, with great punctuality, they were waiting to greet him at the gate. He described their extraordinary knowing as "uncanny."

In Zimbabwe, officials at Hwange National Park decided to "cull" hundreds of elephants with marksmen shooting them from helicopters. On the day of the slaughter, elephants ninety miles away, near a tourist lodge, vanished. They were found bunched together in the corner of the sanctuary farthest from Hwange National Park.

> **Albert Einstein called psychic ability "spooky action at a distance."**

Theoretical physicist Harold Puthoff, director of a government-sponsored remote-viewing project, studied psychics. He said that consciousness stretches far beyond our brains, which have a vast potential for nonlocal (outside time and space) awareness. When perceiving in an extrasensory way, psychics never went anywhere to engage an internal vision of something a thousand miles away. They gained access to a profound connection by viewing it "as no longer other." It requires inner access to a spaceless, timeless dimension where we are all one.

Elephants' mysterious perceptions that defy human logic were clear during the 2004 tsunami. They heroically snatched people up as they rushed to higher ground. In Thailand, Ning Nong, a young elephant who had been on the beach with a handler, rescued eight-year-old Amber Owen and rushed her to higher ground before the killer wave hit. They are loving, wise, and peaceful. Perhaps the telepathic abilities of elephants come from their rootedness in the Earth and their collective sense of self.

A matriarch, Big Tuskless, died in Amboseli National Park and researcher Cynthia Moss brought the jawbone to her camp and placed it among others. After a few days, Big Tuckless's family passed through camp and made a beeline to her jaw. Silently, respectfully, they caressed their matriarch's bones. After the others left, one stayed a long time, stroking, fondling, and turning the jaw over. He was her seven-year-old son.

Iain Douglas-Hamilton moved part of the skeleton of an elephant who had been shot by a farmer to a different location. When the elephant's family came near, they caught the scent and wheeled toward the bones. Trunks waving up and down, ears half out, they seemed hesitant. They advanced in a circle, sniffing and examining the bones. They rocked some with their feet until they clonked together and tasted some. Many carried parts away.

Nearly one hundred years ago, Psychologist William James wrote, "Our lives are like islands in the sea, or like trees in the forest. The maple and the pine may whisper to each other with their leaves but the trees also commingle their roots in the darkness underground…there is a continuum against which our individuality builds but accidental fences."

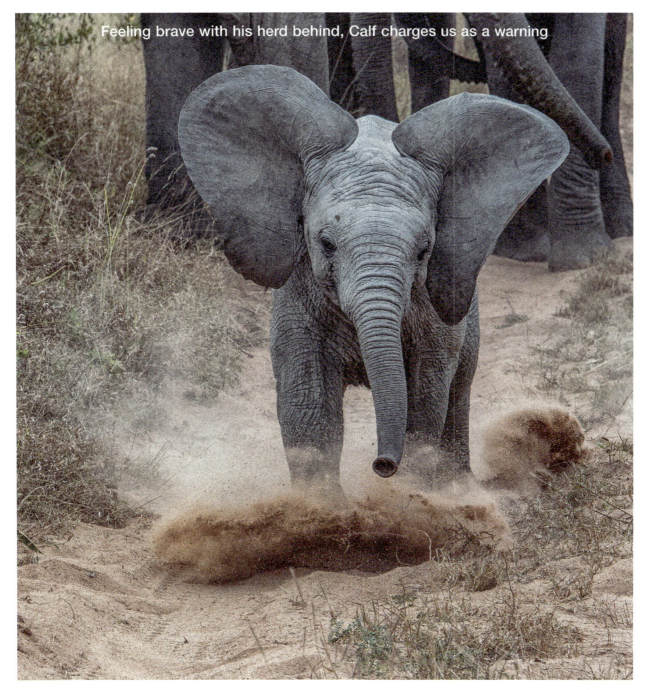
Feeling brave with his herd behind, Calf charges us as a warning

Elephants tap into wisdom greater and deeper than human intelligence. Unlike us, they don't conceive of themselves as separate from other creatures or from the vast universal mind. Love melts away the boundaries between self and others and may explain elephants' extraordinary knowing.

PSYCHOLOGICAL EXTINCTION

What happens when a species goes extinct? Lyall Watson describes the last elephant in Knysna on the cliffs of South Africa's seacoast. Watson was watching a whale lunge and splash. When it was submerged, the reverberations kept coming. He followed the strange rhythm in the air and across the gorge. There, a massive lone elephant stood under a tree. The matriarch, who had been vibrating the Earth and air, had come to the ocean, because it was the nearest source of infrasound. The ocean erupted, and her friend surged heavenward, and spun with her blowhole visible. Her companion rumbled a greeting. This wise grandmother, the largest land animal, had befriended a whale, the largest marine animal. There were no more of her kind. The great ladies commiserated and kept each other company.

Lone elephants are vulnerable to predators, so family is crucial for female elephants. One wonders how her psyche changed as she watched all of her own kind die. Her friendship with the whale speaks of a desolate loneliness.

Although elephants still have the same abilities, psychologically they are changing. Many elephants in the wild have PTSD from having been shot or having watched a family member die from a poisoned arrow. Corrupt governments, Chinese syndicates, local tribes, and trophy hunters have them surrounded. Nowhere is safe. They have startle responses, depression, and hyper-aggression. Their journeys to water and salt supplements used to be a calm float. Now they gallop up on their toes, chronically stressed. They are terrorized by thunder, which sounds like gunshots.

As they drink, the water reflects back their fluid face with a trunk constantly lifting, smelling for danger. Ancient monoliths of a dying species, they survive by running. As herbivores they have no reason to kill except defense, confusion, and panic. At African game parks, tourists who pursued them to get up-close photos were attacked. All animals have a comfort zone of how close a stranger can come before they become alarmed. When their space was invaded, they tried to protect themselves and were shot by the park's rangers.

Can we blame the elephants? Their low-frequency communications with other families alert them to nearby slaughters. They discover hacked-up bodies and scatter buzzards to explore face bones and tusks in a meditative, haunting recognition of friends. Terrorized, stumbling out of war zones, with disrupted social bonds, they are expected to be passive decorations peered at by tourists in Land Rovers. Their habitats have been pushed into isolated islands surrounded

by human population. Under constant stress to find food and water, they trample and eat crops and then are killed by hostile farmers.

As Dr. G. A. Bradshaw, author of *Elephants on the Edge*, says, elephants are undergoing "psychological extinction." Their majestic bodies are the same, but their psyches have scant resemblance to those of free-roaming elephants in previous decades.

Most of the big tuskers have already been killed. In early May 2014, Mountain Bull's GPS-GSM collar stopped moving. He was killed with poison spears in Mt. Kenya National Park after having survived eight gunshot wounds. Four footprints near his body indicated the killers fled to Mozambique. At forty-six, he was six tons, and in his prime. In 2012, to make him less attractive to poachers, veterinarians sawed off a third of his six-and-a-half-foot tusks. He used his uncanny knowledge to evade them but eventually was darted. An undaunted explorer, he tiptoed over, crawled under, broke down and unlocked fences. He led a herd through the migration corridor under a highway that opened up the traditional elephant migratory routes. Although legendary for his resilience, he did not have more than nine lives.

Filmmaker Mark Deeble described seeing Satao, who managed to stay alive by making no predicable visits to watering holes and by staying hidden most of the day. The first sight of him was just a glint in a bush. After two glimmers, the filmmaker realized that he'd seen ivory bouncing off sunlight. When the elephant materialized through the haze, he moved toward water by zigzagging from bush to bush, hiding his tusks and scenting the air for danger. The next time Deeble saw him, there were two wounds in his flank. Poachers had targeted him, but he was still alive, mainly because he knew his huge tusks put him in danger.

On May 30, 2014, shortly after Mountain Bull was poached, Satao was killed by a poison arrow in his left flank. The cardio-toxin coursed through his system, and he collapsed with his legs splayed out. Soon his face was cut off by poachers. Deeble would explain that torrential rain created mud wallows and an Eden for elephants at the southern boundary of Tsavo, which is notorious for poachers because it has only one ranger post. Satao accompanied some other bulls there, and it was a fatal decision.

In a drought, families with older matriarchs with knowledge of watering holes survive, while younger families perish. Older females use their toenails to make steps in an embankment when a calf has fallen in and can't get out. Their wealth of parenting knowledge for young mothers dies with them.

In 1990, a wise matriarch, Echo, gave birth to a baby who could not straighten his forelegs and could barely nurse. He shuffled on wrists and doctors worried they would get infected from the abrasions of walking.

Echo slowed her pace as he hobbled along exhausted, raised him up when he fell and constantly watched his progress. His sister lifted him up to suckle, and they did not give up on him. Echo's wisdom paid off. On the third day, he leaned back and placed his bent soles on the ground and carefully straightened all four legs. Although he fell several times, by day four he was walking normally.

One of my adopted orphans, Kamok, was abandoned because she could not keep up. Eventually, at the orphanage, her legs became stronger, but her family gave up on her. Most likely, no one in Kamok's family had Echo's wisdom. Because older elephants have longer tusks and are poached, infants are raised by inexperienced single mothers. They do not have the support of a herd and knowledge of plants or watering holes. They are expatriates in their own lands.

THE ELEPHANT HOLOCAUST

Elie Wiesel, a survivor of the Jewish Holocaust, wonders why, when prisoners of the death camps so desperately needed help, the world was so silent. "The opposite of love is not hate, but indifference," he told me. "The opposite of life is not death but indifference to life and to death."

I interviewed him at Boston University where he tries to rouse the world from self-concern and indifference and shouts with his "small voice, maybe only heard by a few" to a relatively deaf world. His office, adorned only with a clock and books, is austere, stark and serious. He asks, "How could human beings *imagine* something like that and then *do* it?" Sadness shows in his eyes, big black holes of it, and leaves a trace on his smile.

The questions he asks reverberate deep within the listener and, since much of his thinking is dialectical, he offers no neat solutions. Reminiscent of Hitler's view of himself as the master race, those who view themselves as the master species turn the smartest, most loving mammals in the world into trinkets no one needs. Mothers, daughters, sons, and families are butchered and turned into statues on a shelf.

How can human beings *imagine* something like that and then *do* it? And why can't the rest of us *stop* them?

The elephant genocide is a symbol of civilization gone awry. Human greed has turned their short, sweet lives into dust, but we still remember their faces, all smiles and wrinkles. As light goes out of their eyes, they are miner's canaries sending out alarms about our treatment of other species with whom we share the same breathing Earth.

Playing the Butchery Forward

After terrorist gangs massacre a family of elephants, they unleash more violence on human populations. The illegal wildlife trade is the world's fourth largest criminal activity, with annual profits of $20 billion. Sophisticated networks deal in drugs and arms, take hostages on the open seas, and finance bombings and airplane sabotage.

Sometimes, the poachers are uneducated men with nothing to lose except their lives. A reporter for the Dodo interviewed John Kaimoi after he had served a three-year jail sentence for killing elephants. "When I threw the spear into the animal, that's when it screams. That was my target, so I continued my business." He then took the tusks to cartels in Mombasa. He got $58 per kilogram, and the kingpins then sold it for $1,800 per kilo. Dirt-poor Kenyans, like Kaimoi, get a small fraction of the profits.

Extremists use ivory to bankroll terror. Forty percent of Al Shababa's army, who bombed the Nairobi mall in 2013, is financed by blood ivory. Criminals spread fear and instability in African communities. They have killed over 1200 rangers in thirty-six countries. Rangers are no match for the rocket-propelled grenades and helicopters of the terrorists.

Poachers turn weapons of war against elephants who have done nothing to deserve the monstrous things done to them. Convicted Kenyan poacher John Sumoko, who spent a year in jail for slaughtering seventy elephants, says, "My attacks were so frequent that the elephants could not mate or have calves. There were not enough male elephants." In his graphic descriptions of their anguished screams, the calves' terror after he killed their mothers, and how he separated ivory from the bone, he shows no compassion for the lives upon which he inflicted suffering and pain. He does brag about his "experienced" skills outsmarting those who tried to get away.

John Burnett, of National Public Radio, asked a Tanzania poacher, Mkanga, if he knew that elephants mourn their dead. He shifted in his plastic chair, adjusted his Safari Beer cap, and smirked, "Sometimes when they have a funeral, it's like a party for me," he said. "You shoot one, and before he dies the others come to mourn for the one who is injured. And so I kill another one, and kill another one." Ten guys with high-powered rifles slaughter elephants, who don't have a chance. It is just a means of easy cash and affirming their own power. In South Africa, Kenya, Tanzania, and Mozambique, traders come late at night with the police and military to buy ivory from poachers. Countries attempt to stop poaching, but corruption makes it difficult.

Justin, an ivory trafficker who moves half a million dollars of illegal ivory per year in Cameroon, was interviewed by a reporter. He spoke proudly of his supply chain—created by bribes—used to bring ivory to his Chinese partners. Reporter Damon Tabor asked him, "What's going to happen when there are no elephants left?"

"In Africa, animals are animals," he chuckled. He said his girlfriend has a dog and he told her if the dog were in Africa, "I would use it for a nice pepper sauce."

Poachers hack off the live part, a loving, wise mother, and keep the dead part, the ivory. Although blood ivory from recently killed elephants is illegal, smugglers use tea or paint to made it look aged. Reporters posing as customers have filmed the staff at Chinese Arts and Crafts in Hong Kong admitting they export raw blood ivory to mainland China, then import it back as carved ivory, which is illegal. They openly disseminate smuggling tips, such as carving ivory in the shape of an apple and painting it red and mingling ivory chopsticks with plastic ones to fool customs officials.

Human Vanity Fuels the Slaughters

In America and Europe, women used to view fur coats as glamorous, but now wearing fur is considered a sign of insensitivity to the animals who lost their lives. Animal rights groups have documented how minks and foxes are stuck in cages their whole lives and that documentation has changed the meaning of wearing fur.

In generations past, white men have exploited African nations by enslaving people. Like elephants, slaves were targets of massive violence. The king of Belgium was famous for mutilating the hands and feet of slaves in the Congo. Culls and translocations to strange lands also shattered families. Eventually global distaste for slavery put slave traders out of business.

Gradually, ivory may become a symbol of butchery and baby elephants left to die. It is human vanity to value ivory chopsticks more than the mother and baby who died for them. An ivory carver could never make an elephant.

Prominent Chinese citizens—Li Bingbing, Jackie Chan, Jiang Wen, Yao Ming, and some top Asian CEOs—are getting the message out to the Asian masses. When the cultured Chinese shun ivory, its price will drop. To save elephants, the carvers could begin to carve vegetable ivory, made from the tagua nut. It grows on palm trees in the Amazon basin in Bolivia, Ecuador, and Peru. A tagua palm produces the same amount of "ivory" as one female elephant. Once it is carved and polished, many people cannot distinguish it from elephant ivory.

It is a race between public opinion and demand, and it may end with wild elephants turned into statues. As a blogger on the Yao Ming Foundation website says, "I hope the ivory trade is banished…We need to have mercy on these majestic treasures of the earth."

Pygmy Elephant in Borneo. They are rarely poached because there is less corruption.

THE TRUE ORPHANS

In Hoedspruit, South Africa, I interviewed a game ranger who used to kill hippos. He could no longer do so after Jessica, a newborn hippo calf, swept up onto his riverbank during the flood of the Blyde River.

On March 11, 2000, when the debris in his yard began moving, Tony Joubert discovered a premature hippo baby with an umbilical cord attached. Clearly, she would not survive on her own. Tony made some milk from eggs and cream, and Jessica took to the bottle. She quickly became part of his family, including his wife and their pets, ZaZa, a Rottweiler and bull terriers.

The Jouberts thought of her as a daughter. When she got older, she mingled with wild hippos and was attacked. They nursed her wounds by rubbing massage oils on her nightly. She swims with wild friends during the day but, come evening, her barrel shape with stubby legs waddles home. She noses her huge mouth onto the kitchen counter, opens wide, and her family drops in two loaves of bread, sweet potatoes, and pounds of carrots. She watches television but is not allowed on the sofa, because she crushes it. Her bed, which she has broken five times, is on the verandah. During the night, eight or nine hippos visit her. Tony says they are a great security system. He leaves his keys in the car and doesn't lock the house. In the morning, Tony shares his coffee with her, but she likes Rooibos sweet tea better. She helps with chores by mowing the grass and trimming the bushes.

As a ranger, Tony once culled 1,700 starving hippos in Zambia. Once he fell in love with Jessica, he could no longer kill any hippos. His wife says, "Jessica taught him much better values." He is hoping Jessica will give birth to a calf and he'll help her raise it, the way a grandfather might.

Tony says his "fantastic bond" with Jessica makes him realize how we underestimate animals. Back when he culled hippos, he did not empathize with their happiness and distress. Because of his love of Jessica, an animal became someone, not something. Destroying animals was a grim part of his job. He never enjoyed it. He still has the power to play God, but love made it impossible.

We need to have compassion for the psychological damage of trophy hunters. If causing death and suffering gives a person joy, in a deep psychic region, a light has gone out. As St. Paul wrote, they "see through a glass darkly." It must be painful to be so impotent, you get power from crushing the life out of another living creature.

As Abraham Lincoln said, "If you want to test a man's character, give him power." Animals are at our mercy. What we do with our power to hurt them illustrates a person's internal landscape. Urges to destroy beauty come from feelings of ugliness. A desire to maim, mutilate, and suffocate comes from internal rage. A lack of mercy and kindness come from a dark, barren abyss.

Laws enable wealthy Americans to act out their character flaws upon the innocent, because human law is made by humans, for humans. Both animals and many poor people have no voice. Although animals have as much right to life as we do, they can't defend themselves from guns. When poor people in Africa hunt to feed their families, they are jailed for poaching, but when rich Americans slaughter animals for fun, it is legal.

Our country was shamed when six hunters on a lethal ego trip shot an endangered rhino and draped an American flag on his lifeless corpse. Outraged by desecrating our flag in such a perverted manner, protesters took to their keyboards. "Real men risk their lives to protect these amazing creatures." "How long did it take all six of you to shoot a slow moving animal the size of a small building with a high-powered rifle?"

In the gloat photo some had guns slung on their shoulders. One is in the hump position with his leg up on the rump of the rhino, showing dominance the way dogs do. It is pure self-delusion to believe that six men with weapons did anything manly by this cruel act.

Some trophy hunters say they are conservationists—that they care about animals. This sounds like a fairy tale, concocted by hunting groups.

No matter how they rationalize killing animals to save them, social media tells the real story. Jimmy John Liautaud, mogul of the Chicago-based sandwich chain, sits on the front leg of a dead elephant and reaches forward with two thumbs up, smiling proudly at the camera.

One imagines the scene. The grandmotherly elephant is twisting a branch with her trunk and stuffing leaves in her mouth. She happily chews while her trunk reaches down to caress a calf leaning against her. The calf, whose gait is wobbly, reaches up to suckle.

Liautaud drives up in a truck with a handful of guides. One positions the sandbag for his rifle and another prepares his "sundowner," the drink he will have in celebration. Liautaud rests his gun on the support and leans down to see through the scope. Her huge maternal shape fills the frame. It would be impossible to miss the elephant, who is chewing, looking at him.

Liautaud pulls the trigger. The gun booms. The elephant screams and crumples to her knees. The calf shrieks. The branch falls out of her mouth, a pink cavity full of leaf fragments, and gasps. Her head falls onto the ground. Blood pumps out of her shoulder. The calf bellows and trips over his trunk, scampering into the bushes. He gets away from the menace of the men but can't leave the scene, because he is lost without his mother.

The sandwich mogul slaps a high-five to his team. They all clink glasses, toasting his courage to the tortured gasps of the matriarch. Over their congratulations—"Way to go. Nice shot. Well done"—is the sound of her gurgling. She fights to live with a terrible hissing effort for thirty minutes.

If the orphaned calf can overcome his innocence enough to evade predators, he will die from emaciation in three weeks. Without his mother, he will never taste the wonders of the world. But the true orphan is Liautaud, who also wiped out the last living female rhino and her unborn calf in the Mangetti National Park in Nambia.

Other beings love life. They did not evolve through centuries to be slaughtered for a thrill. Only human arrogance makes their lives less important. Those who hurt animals to act out power fantasies have lost connection to Mother Earth, who values all life.

A common picture of a trophy hunter is of the "hunter" sitting on the lion's neck, pulling back his prey's jaw to show the fangs. "Look at me. I'm a real man to have killed this big-toothed animal."

On another level, he knows he's kidding himself. There's no danger in a canned hunt. The lion, who was orphaned because trophy hunters shot his mother, was never taught to hunt. He was petted as a cub until he got bigger. Kept in a cage like a farmyard chicken his whole life, one day he is dragged by his back feet out of the cage and thrown into a larger enclosure. The lion is confused by the new, bigger space and sniffs around to check out the new digs.
There's a challenge to finding him but not to slaughtering him, because he does not confront his attacker. Sometimes he is drugged to make the kill easier.

By a trick of the mind, the shooter manages to believe the lion was the scary one, not himself. What's scary is that he is out of control. Trophy hunting is addictive, leading to more and more kills. Hippos and alligators are shot from the safety of boats. But in the gloat photo, the hunter props open their mouths to expose their large teeth. "Look how brave I am to have killed this ferocious animal."

Another photo is of a "hunter" mounted way back on the lion's back. It's the position of one dog showing dominance by humping another. The humper pulls the cat's face up by a fistful of mane. He seems to take shallow breaths to quell the stench of death.

The hunter silences that famous MGM roar and destroys the dignity of an icon of strength.

After he drains the life out of the lion, he moves into the spotlight for a selfie. Does he think this makes him a real man? Only self-delusion enables him to believe he was brave. It's like

a Revolutionary or Civil War reenactment, but it's more exciting because real bullets are fired and live beings are killed.

In 2011, Donald Trump, Jr. and his brother, Eric, went on a safari killing spree in Zimbabwe. Among the many animals they slaughtered were a kudu, a civet cat, a buffalo, a crocodile, a leopard, and an elephant. Donald Trump, Jr., thirty-four years old, held the elephant's tail and smiled at the camera. With a strand of bullets strung around his waist, like a real hunter, and with a bloody knife clutched in his hand, he stood by the carcass looking proud.

Trump rationalized his brutal behavior by saying his hunting fees fed villagers and helped communities. According to a report by a group of economists, most hunting revenue goes to rich, white landowners, with only 3 percent trickling down to the local people. Conservationists say that hunting camp owners sell the meat by the kilo to a market, so only those with funds benefit from the meat.

Wildlife filmmaker Dereck Joubert corrected the basic assumptions of hunters. A male lion killed by a hunter earns around $23,000, but his potential future value is destroyed by the bullet. If he is kept alive for photographers and tourists to photograph, over his lifetime he will earn $2,000,000 through safari companies and lodges who provide jobs to and buy supplies from the community. He will also be able to father cubs, who will earn the same amount. The value of wildlife as an eco-tourism asset is far greater than what hunters pay to hang a severed head on a wall. Saying they are conservationists is a rationalization of those on lethal ego trips. "Like all animals, elephants, buffalo, and crocodiles deserve better than to be killed and hacked apart for two young millionaires' grisly photo opportunity," said a spokesperson for People for the Ethical Treatment of Animals.

When Britt St. John jumped in a reservoir at Paltz, New York, to save a drowning fawn, he said, "I felt joy to save a life. I felt lucky to be there." Similarly, in Davidson, Michigan, firemen with a tractor rescued a pregnant mare from a frozen lake. In Detroit, Michigan, Rick Swoat ignored fears for his own safety and jumped into a moat at a zoo to save a drowning chimpanzee. Eldad, with Hope for Paws, rescues dogs in Los Angeles. He climbs through sewer systems to bribe starving and injured strays with cheeseburgers, takes them for medical attention, food, water, and love. These and the keepers who raise orphaned elephant babies are real men. They know the peace of giving, the light-heartedness of kindness, and are connected to something beyond themselves. Life for them is a brotherhood and sisterhood where all life is precious.

One famous poacher, who also enjoys hacking animals apart, is American dentist Walter Palmer. His Zimbabwe guides tied a dead animal to the back of their vehicle and lured Cecil, a beautiful, black-maned lion with twelve cubs to protect, out of a safe area in Hwange National Park.

They chose him because he was massive, a warrior with big black chunks of dreadlocks. They shined a spotlight on Cecil to blind him, then Palmer shot him with a bow and arrow. Cecil was injured from the first shot but escaped and fought to live for forty-four hours while the crew tracked him and killed him. Palmer, who paid $55,000 for the grisly privilege, cut off Cecil's head and extracted his teeth for trophies. The team then tried to destroy the GPS tracking collar, probably visible when they led him out of the park and into the spotlights before the kill. Palmer butchered an Oxford University research subject and had no permit to do so. Palmer, who also killed a rhino, had a previous felony in Wisconsin. Similarly, he poached a bear in an unauthorized zone, lied to cover his crime, and offered fellow hunters $22,000 to lie for him. Palmer's wife, Tonette, has seven licenses for sport hunting. They produced another "hunter." Natalie Palmer is in a gloat photo in a truck with three wolves she killed. Their eyes gaze vacantly, bodies crumpled. She is holding the bloody mouth of one, pulling the lips back. She attempts to show the wolf's huge teeth, but his tongue hangs over the side of his jaw, oozing blood. In life, he was beautiful. She transformed him into a replica of her—gruesome and ghastly. The glee in her eyes is like that of Jack Nicholson's character in *The Shining*. As one keyboard comment says, "OMG, he bred himself."

On Palmer's estate are blinds from which to shoot unsuspecting deer and a killing room with fifty heads of rare animals from his macabre addiction. Palmer's treatment of his victims mirrors those of serial killer Jeffrey Dahmer. In a 1994 interview, Dahmer told Stone Phillips that he first took trophies from dogs and cats he slaughtered. When he graduated to humans, he looked for the best-looking guy. Fueled by lust and a desire for complete control, he dismembered them. Similarly, Palmer found a gorgeous lion to butcher. When holding up the body from another handsome victim, a leopard, Palmer is bare-chested, his skin absorbing the blood of his kill.

Just as pornography is used by serial killers to increase violent fantasies, hunting magazines picture successful hunters in dominant poses. An essay by Gareth Patterson, which compares trophy hunters with serial killers, found many similarities. In addition to the addictive quality of both, souvenirs are taken to relive the thrill. Their crimes are both premeditated and they both view their prey as objects.

The film *On Frozen Ground* was based on the true story of Robert Hansen, a big game hunter in Alaska, who also hunted and killed twenty prostitutes. He pointed his gun at the women and told them to take off their clothes and run through the snow. Then, similar to canned lion hunts, they were given a start and were stalked before they were shot. In this elaborate game, the prey had no possibility of survival. Like Palmer, he also sometimes used a crossbow. There's not much difference between the serial killing of animals and the serial killing of people.

In 2013, in Hwange National Park, near where Cecil was murdered, the worst massacre of elephants in Southern Africa in twenty-five years took place. Poachers poisoned the water supply and killed 300 elephants for their tusks. The cyanide in the water also killed zebra, buffalo, impala, and many other animals. Then all the animals who fed on the carcasses died—lions, hyenas, and vultures. Several villagers and police, who were bribed to ignore the poachers, were arrested. None of them were willing to identify the foreign kingpins who bought the ivory. To gobble up some easy cash, they wiped out the web of life around them. Similarly, on December 7, 2014, in Hwange National Park, soldiers in helicopters and trucks began firing shots to separate baby elephants from their mothers. Blasts, smoke, dust, wind, voices, helicopter blades, and vehicles pushed the screaming families away from terrified toddlers. The soldiers then kidnapped sixty calves. Animal groups pleaded with the government to return the babies to their families. They argued that the calves could not emotionally thrive without their mothers. However, However, Zimbabwe officials, their hearts hardened with avarice, sold the babies to China.

Many were not surprised with Robert Mugabe's blatant disregard of animal welfare. Prime Minister of Zimbabwe, Mugabe made international headlines on March 1, 2015. "Robert Mugabe eats a zoo for 'obscene 91st birthday,'" the *Independent* announced. In his million-dollar birthday bash, he cooked and served elephant, as well as lion and crocodile. Mugabe has more power than he knows how to use wisely. He views other species as his property and loots his country's wildlife for his lavish lifestyle.

In July 2015, eight months after their abduction, twenty-four calves were sent by Zimbabwe to Chimelong Park for a life in captivity. Conservationists said tourists who pay to view the babies in forced isolation will only see a stupefied body. The personality of the calf will be dampened by depression and trauma. Of the four elephants sold to China in 2012, one of them has already died. Jason Bell, of the International Fund for Animal Rescue, said he was "sickened." Millions of animal lovers worldwide were appalled that babies were used as commodities, saying that the calves belong to their families, to nature.

Three injured calves—one missing a tail and another a part of a trunk—escaped what conservationists called a "life of servitude." Because of their imperfections, they were sent to the Zimbabwe Elephant Nursery in Harare for rehabilitation and eventual return to the wild. "Out of tragedy," one reader posted on Facebook, "comes a small ray of light."

National Geographic posted secret photos of the calves at Chimelong Park. Taken by Chunmei Hu, a project manager for Nature University in Beijing, they show deep wounds and abrasions, sunken faces, lackluster skin, and signs of malnourishment. "Most of the injuries are consistent with bullhook wounds," said Joyce Poole, cofounder of Elephant Voices. Bullhooks are poker-like metal instruments used to strike young elephants to break their spirits.

Scott Blais, of the Global Sanctuary for Elephants, who once worked in the captive elephant industry, believes some of the wounds are from infighting. At such a young age, "these

elephants need to be consoled, comforted, and protected." Instead, their captive environment leaves a void for healthy emotional, psychological, and physical development. "They've already started to lose empathy for one another. Humans are taking away everything that is fundamentally 'elephant.'"

People who slaughter animals for fun and profit are the true orphans. The world's music is not theirs to silence. They do not own animals any more than they own sunshine or rain. They have stepped out of nature and are separate from the source from which they came, Mother Earth.

Native hunters had a closer spiritual relationship with animals, because all creatures were in their web of life. The healing of the planet rests on us seeing that an elephant's suffering, a rhino's suffering, a lion's suffering is everyone's suffering. An elephant's eyes reflect our own essence back to us. We can inhale the elephant's exhaled air and know we are all part of the same breathing Earth. With empathic engagement, we know they are not objects of our purposes.

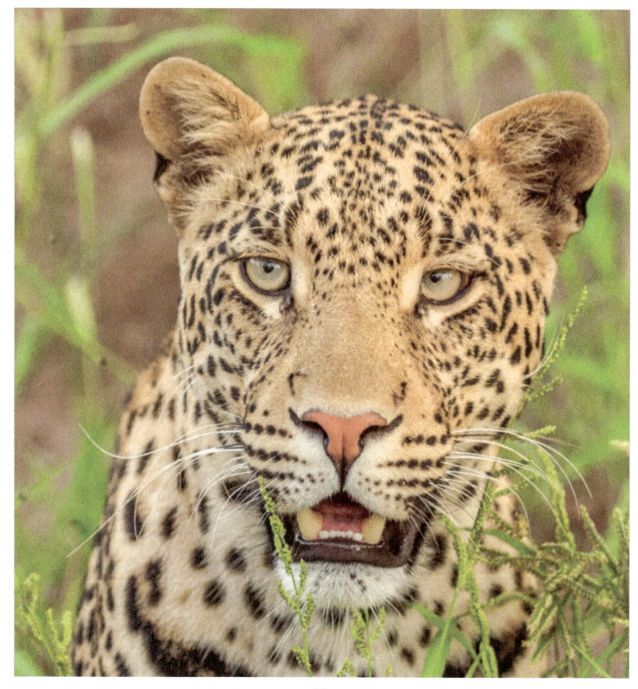

MOTHER EARTH

A herd of elephants, vast and alive with muscle and bone, is like a moving mountain. Heads like warriors' shields, skin creased with age, strides steady and deliberate are so utterly of the Earth. Their grandmotherly wisdom, their peaceful nurturing, are like nature herself. On their watch, the world lasted because they take only what they need.

On our watch, we destroy our environment by taking more than we need. As Daphne Sheldrick says, "Humans are the endangered species, because we have stepped out of nature and jeopardized our own survival."

The indulgences of our expanding civilization are digging our grave. We are just one species of our mother, whose nurturing has breathed life into millions of brother and sister species. She hugs us with sunshine, tickles us with sand squishing between our toes, and kisses us with rain. All animals, including us, are in her embrace. We are a family. We share the same home. But our family is in crisis. We have multiplied so rapidly that we took our brothers' and sister's land and resources. What is left of their territories has been cut up with roads. In Africa, savannas have been cleared for agriculture. Pastoralists are overgrazing livestock on land reserved for buffalo, zebra, elephants, and lions. Farms and ranches push animals into small areas. When they venture out to find food and eat crops, they are killed. Mbegu, who got separated from her stampeding family, was brutally stabbed by villagers. One of my elephant babies, Naipoki, fell down a well and was mauled by predators. We construct human conveniences without protecting them from their dangers, and we do not want to share the land we took from them.

In America, forests can't hold out to pizza franchises. Those animals whose homes are destroyed can't find berries, nuts, water, and partners with whom to make babies. When they do find a mate to start a family, they can't build nests, because the trees were bulldozed over. When they look for food in yards where their territory used to be, they are seen as pests and scared away. We view the abundance of our mother as our own.

Most people do not purposely hurt animals, but we take what they need to survive, because we have the power to do so. Over half of other species have died in the past forty years. And the losses are accelerating.

Pope Francis has been vocal about our destruction of other species. "Because of us," he said, "thousands of species will no longer give glory to God by their very existence, nor convey their message to us. We have no such right."

The story of Noah is about how God was so upset by human wickedness that he flooded people off the Earth. He made sure all the animals, two by two, got safely in the ark. I always took this story as a myth, but people in Mesha Naxuan, Turkey, found evidence of an ark in a mudslide after a volcano erupted. It was the exact dimensions mentioned in the Bible. Outside were thousands and thousands of graves of what some believe were the wicked. Now all animals are in mortal danger, and we are the flood. Elephants, rhinos, and lions may not make it into the ark.

Without reverence for the antlered, tailed, and amber-eyed, they will perish. Messages in whiffs and scents make their present moment vast. The fluid element of air bends leaves and brings the smell of deer, vibrations of thunder, the smell of rain. Their survival depends on seeing a spotted face through a bush, sensing a change in humidity, a scent in urine.

We no longer hear the multiple tongues of the cosmos—smells of residents of the forest, vibrations from the ground, croaking of frogs, flickering of fireflies, the majestic turn of the seasons.

The more we insulate ourselves from the Earth's enchantment, the less we value our brother and sister species. Our ancestors navigated their shimmering world of beauty and hazard and were attuned to every flicker of a tail in grass. Somewhere deep in our psyche their ghosts are wired to respond to nature.

These ghosts came alive in me out in the African bush, after we'd left the grid of power lines and the exclusively human world. In a Land Rover, we followed a leopard on a hunt. He crossed a stream, then the spotted phantom vaporized into trees for a lookout. After targeting some impala, he descended into bushes, his spots mingling with tangled limbs. His cushioned feet moved as silently and delicately as a dancer's. Only an ambush would catch the swift-footed impala.Up ahead, the impalas' heads bent in feeding. The leopard was out of the bush, slithering through grass, on his belly. Head low, green glades brushed his whiskers and blinked his eyes as he crawled. Shoulders, like pistons, rippled his skin taut. I held my breath, every cell on high alert. The wind carried the musty decay of the long dead, but did it carry the scent of the leopard, closer to erupting into fangs and claws?

He wasn't invisible to the baboons. They shrieked an alarm. Impalas heads jerked up, eyes widened, ears cupped, they barked a warning. He marched in the open. His feet, no longer dainty, stamped up dust while squirrels and other creatures called alarms. The impalas' eyes and ears followed him, as well as our vehicle with many moving heads, arms, and cameras. We stayed back a respectful distance as he climbed an acacia tree. He stretched out on a branch listening to the panic. Birds sent warnings to monkeys, squirrels, and wart hogs, radiating out in concentric circles. Finally, they stopped.

Then he leaped down and sauntered over to our huge metal body with big rubber feet. Six huge cameras eyed him, click, click, click. He smelled our tires, rubbed against our vehicle, then slithered over to me at the side of the truck.

He peered up and leaned forward as if to say, "I couldn't help but notice that you are stalking me." A foot apart, we held each other by our gaze. I felt his poised alertness in my muscles as our eyes locked. Tiny hairs on the back of my neck lifted as I drank in the flecks of yellow in his eyes.

Dazzled by the chords he struck in me, he harmonized with every cell in my body. An ancient part of us knows his wildness. We share the same life-force. We are both made from blood, bone, and elements from the Earth. His stunning beauty held innocence and sheer vulnerability. My encounter with him was so wide and deep it lasts to this day. It is one of the treasures in my heart, which broke when I saw the photo of Walter Palmer holding the limp body of a gorgeous leopard killed for a trophy. That fragility I felt seemed a premonition. It's hard for me to grasp going to Africa to pillage and plunder the beauty there.

Africa brought me back to a childish sense of wonder. I came home to myself. Every morning, the sun lit the horizon with fire, rimmed the arms of trees, then blazed orange, yellow, and pink all over the landscape like flowers blooming. The present was fuller and the future full of unexpected possibilities. The jungle veiled what was ahead in the road—always a surprise. What I expected to happen did not happen. Sometimes I was awestruck.

I dreaded the horror of a kill when a lioness saved a just-born wildebeest from hyenas. The lioness kept her wobbly meal by her side, as hyenas clambered around, perhaps waiting to scavenge leftovers.

The lioness lunged at them, and they fled.

Knock-kneed, quivering, still-wet from the afterbirth, the gnu snuggled into the lion looking for warmth and milk. Fragile, but with a powerful urge to live in her tiny heart, the baby rubbed noses with the lion before moving up to suckle the lion's ear. At the moment of death, something miraculous happened. The lion's mothering instinct took over.

Instead of eating the baby, the lion licked her head, cuddled and comforted her. They lay under the trees in soft grass, huddled against each other, caressing. Love flowed between predator and prey. The baby was so innocent; she did not know the lion could eat her. Perhaps the lioness had lost her own cubs. The lioness sensed the helpless newborn's need to press up against another who is gentle and loving. Some wisdom made the tiny wildebeest bigger than her biological existence as food. After a while, the lion's attention turned back to the Serengeti. She rose to hunt. As the calf walked away, the lioness watched.

Glimpsing love where violence might have been left me amazed. Some reverence for life took over. Some primordial wisdom saved the baby.

We have a great hunger for grace. We look for ways to water, fertilize, and nourish it. By connecting with other creatures with whom we share the planet, we nourish wonder.

Paul Nicklen, a *National Geographic* photographer, tells a similar story about mothering. Deep in our cellular memory, we know we are all connected. When he traveled to Antarctica to photograph leopard seals, his guide spotted the biggest one he'd ever seen. "Time to get in the watta, ya?" the guide asked.

The blond-haired, oceanic-eyed Nicklen finished suiting up his scuba gear, jumped out of the safety of the zodiac, and descended into icy water. Nicklen moved toward the gray submarine shape cautiously. A skilled huntress, the seal was a vicious predator.

The seal dropped the penguin she'd caught and swam over to investigate the strange bubbly creature with the glass face and rubber fins. Opening her mouth, larger than a grizzly bear's, around the photographer's head and camera, the seal examined her visitor. Nicklin's legs trembled; his mouth was dry. Though terrified, he continued to click the camera—capturing the seal's sharp teeth, blotches on the roof of the mouth, and her spotted underbelly.

After her display of threat, the seal swam away, grabbed a live penguin, and offered it to her guest. When Nicklen didn't take the penguin, the seal presented him with a dead penguin. Still her visitor would not eat. The seal shoved penguin flesh into the camera, which looked to her like the photographer's mouth. When the visitor still would not eat, the seal seemed panicked that Nicklen would starve. She tried partly consumed penguin, then penguin eating lessons, which she provided.

For four days, Nicklen visited the seal. He was mothered and nurtured by what he thought was a vicious predator because he let go of assumptions and opened his heart to the seal.

As a child, he grew up with the Inuit of Canada. They didn't watch TV, play video games, or have cell phones but were fascinated by the web of life on the tundra. Perhaps the seal resonated with his reverence for other species. We can all nourish ourselves by opening our hearts to other creatures.

David Abrams, in *The Spell of the Sensuous*, traced how we renounced our animal kinship and cut ourselves off from the Earth. He says the world of predators is too unpredictable for human sensibilities. He says our language creates "a kind of perceptual boundary that hovers, like a translucent veil, between those who speak that language and the sensuous terrain they inhabit." He says we escape the vulnerability of our bodies by living in our minds. Our bodies decay, break down, and die. Animals know the world by living fully in their bodies and senses. We live in theoretical realms, which do not make hairs stand up on the backs of our necks the way a close-by leopard might. He says civilization, which values knowledge from microscopes and computers, has turned in upon itself. We do not sense the universe's vitality when staring at a virtual world.

The real world is crying out for help. Many species are doomed to live in relics of their former homes. In past eras, our goal was to conquer nature, bend it to our will. That was when wilderness was wild, but now wildlife must be protected from the human population explosion.

Loss of Habitats

In 2014, I was on a photography safari in the Maasai Mara in southwest Kenya. We drove into the shallow part of a turbulent river to capture a pride of lions as they crossed. All the adults made it across. Hesitantly, they jumped across on rocks, but the ferociousness of the water, a rumbling cascade splashing against boulders, was daunting.

Two cubs came down and growled at the river. One leaped in and was swept downstream. Tilting his face upward, blinking, he paddled fiercely against the current and arrived at the opposite shore. Hair stuck to his face, water streamed from him, but he dragged himself up and disappeared into brush. The other cub batted the water with his paw then cried squeakily. Between two trees, where the first cub disappeared, mom's head poked out. Her mouth was a thin line. More cries. Rock by rock, she leaped back to her offspring, now partway up a hill. She rubbed against him for comfort, then tried to lift him by the back of the neck. His feet dragged. He dropped. He was too heavy. Mom seemed confused, went to the top of the hill, and surveyed the landscape. Then, to our dismay, she left him there.

Just the evening before, two lion cubs were killed by hyenas because Maasai and their cattle separated the babies from their mothers. The lions couldn't get to their offspring because if they got near the cattle, the Maasai, with their distinctive red dress, beads, and spears, would kill them.

As we left, we assumed the mother knew there was no immediate danger, but that could change. The cub was vulnerable. I felt ashamed. We had been so absorbed in picture taking, we didn't consider how our clicking cameras, people, and truck frightened him. Also, we were in a shallow part of the river easier to cross.

Last seen, he was crying, looking across the river for his mother. And, we had helped put his precious life in danger. The consequences of our self-absorption for this little cub could have been fatal. That's how we cause the death of other species not by intent.

Human civilization is destroying other species, forests, and elements of the biosphere we need to live. The Earth, four and a half billion years old, has been here 22,500 times longer than we have. Against the immensity of mountains, with ocher-orange cliffs, topped by an indigo sky, humans are insignificant specks.

Our lives are held and sustained by Mother Nature, our most primal source of nourishment. If we deplete this womb of bounty, we will become a flimsy dust. Other species will evolve who do not need what we destroy. The Earth will survive our damage, but we may not. As Julia Roberts says, "Nature does not need us, but we need nature."

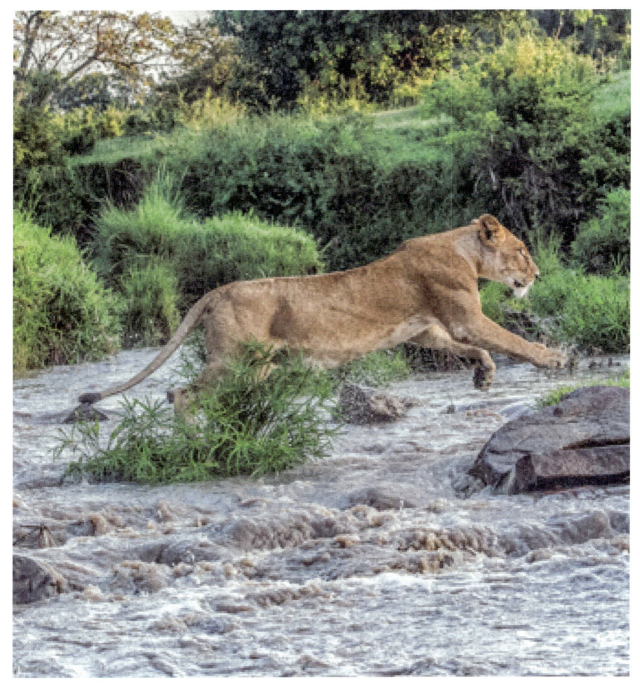

STIRRINGS OF HOPE

Our mistakes are terrible, but our talent is without measure. We can become Earth restorers, not destroyers. We can replace separateness, arrogance, and cruelty with mercy, humility, and kindness.

Like many social movements, the one to help elephants, rhinos, and lions corrects horrific injustices. It is part of a cultural shift in the way we view animals. The burgeoning movement, like a phoenix slowly rising from the ashes of mindless slaughter, is taking root faster than other social movements because of social media.

On October 4, 2014, a groundswell of people reacted to the elephant and rhinoceros holocaust. Thousands marched in 136 cities around the globe to end the killing of elephants and rhinos, ban the sale of ivory and rhino horn, and shut down carving factories. Los Angeles and countries like New Zealand, Scotland, and the Netherlands also marched for lions.

They marched, we marched, because doing nothing will not stop the force of evil, because the opposite of life is not death but indifference to life and to death. We marched because human greed has created senseless suffering for useless trinkets and remedies. We marched because other living creatures are not ours to destroy. They feel love, joy, pain, and grief. Each is someone—not something. We marched for Satao, Mountain Bull, for the matriarch Qumquat killed by poachers, and Hope and Thandi, rhinos hacked up by a machete. We marched for the vulnerable still alive. We marched because heartbreak can challenge us to evolve. Throughout history, grief and injustice have provided an engine for change. We marched because we will not go gentle into the night of extinction.

With signs, chanting, and singing, we marched to give voice to the voiceless. We marched with faith our voices would be heard. As Emily Dickinson said, faith is a fragile, winged thing. We marched so the bird of faith will become an angel of mercy.

Getting Political for Elephants and Rhinos and Lions

Because wildlife crime, ivory, rhino horn, and lion bones fund terrorism, governments are responding. Although the new Kenyan Wildlife Act has harsher penalties for poachers, the old laws in Kenya did not value elephants. The notorious poacher, Pekei ole Shoke, who killed the matriarch Qumquat, had been jailed but then released. He boasted to game rangers who arrested him that he would kill more elephants to pay his fine. A long-term poacher, under the previous laws, he was given freedom to hack Qumquat and her family to death. Eventually on May 15, 2015, Pekei ole Shoke was punished for killing Qumquat and her family. He was given a year in jail, the maximum sentence under the old law, which seems lenient given his atrocities.

The new Kenya Wildlife Conservation and Management Act, operational on January 10, 2014, has ramped up penalties for wildlife crime. On August 28, 2015, two Kenyan men in Narok near the Maasai Mara, were sent to prison for life or to pay $1 million.

In the United States, the Tusker Bill was proposed in honor of Satao, the elephant bull killed in Tsavo East. It is legislation placed before the US Congress that would impose sanctions on countries that do not curb the bloody ivory trade.

On September 25, 2015, President Obama and President Xi Jinping of China pledged to enact a nearly complete ban on ivory imports and exports that would close loopholes that enable illicit trafficking of ivory. Similarly, bipartisan movements are underway in many states to completely ban elephant and rhino horn commerce. Traffickers use tea, iodine, or paint on ivory from recently killed elephants to make it look old. Halting the trade of all ivory is the only way to halt extinction. California, New York, New Jersey, Vermont, Illinois, Massachusetts, Hawaii, Florida, Oklahoma, Virginia, Maryland, Iowa, Connecticut, and Virginia have introduced ivory sales bans. They are designed to eliminate markets and profits from blood ivory.

On March 5, 2015, Ringling Bros. and Barnum and Bailey Circus, because of the "mood shift among our consumers" announced they would phase out elephant acts by 2018. Ken Field, chairman and CEO of Field Entertainment, said he wanted to make sure future generations could see the magnificent animals. "We knew we would play a critical role in saving the endangered Asian elephants for future generations. The elephants will be sent to the Center for Elephant Conservation in Florida.

High-tech, Low-tech

Poachers, funded by criminal syndicates, have cars and helicopters. They wear night-vision goggles and carry high-powered rifles, silencers, electric saws, and tranquilizers. With all the technology used to slaughter wildlife, now some technology protects them. Drones, tiny quiet eyes in the sky, fly aerial surveillance. Alarmed fences can text a message when they've been cut or tampered with.

Computer analysis of slaughters predicts future ones. At the University of Maryland, data from kills tells rangers where to go. At Balule, a small reserve in South Africa, rhinos are usually killed 160 yards from a paved road. Poachers drive around the perimeter fence in the late afternoon to find a nearby animal. As sunset, four poachers return to that spot. They raise the hood to pretend the car is broken. One stays with the car. Three climb the fence, kill the rhino, cut off the horn, and run back to the vehicle in ten minutes. Now rangers and drones patrol the paved roads and record license plate numbers of cars in strategic places. There has been no poaching in Balule in eight months, because they believe there are "eyes in the sky."

Some elephant tusks are being painted with a pink dye that makes the ivory useless to traffickers. Rhinos are being fitted with spy cameras and heart monitors linked to alarms to catch poachers red-handed. Dr. Paul O'Donoghue of Chester University in the UK explained that the alarms pinpoint the attack location so rangers can soon be on the scene.

Tranquilizing an animal in the field is risky because doctors have to guess the rhino's weight to inject the correct dose. It takes time, is costly, and many things can go wrong in the anesthesia process. Throwing technology at poaching has not had huge results and has been at a tremendous cost while the massacres continue.

The low-tech horse has been successful in Chad's Zakouma National Park, where there has been no poaching for three years. Rains flood the park for months, making it inaccessible to vehicles. At the beginning and end of the deluge, poachers on horseback butcher most of the elephants. In 2005, there were about 4000 elephants. Now there are only 450, but none has been poached since 2010. That's when seventy rangers on horseback from local nomadic communities were trained.

Maasai warriors now work in tourist camps and know that the loss of wildlife is a loss of income. They alert rangers about poachers and are being trained as Guardians for lions. They earn a salary to monitor the lions and alert herders where to move cattle to avoid conflict. In the Luangwa Valley in Zambia, 1500 poachers were converted to farmers by Comaco. They surrendered their weapons and snares and were taught beekeeping and farming of peanut butter, soy, and rice.

The story of one of the recruits, Thompson Tembo, shows how criminal gangs exploit poverty. For two large tusks, he was paid $500, split between the poaching gang. The retail price in China is over a million dollars. Now with the profits from farming, he has bought two vehicles, six grinding mills, and soon will have a tractor. "I think about all the elephants I killed," he told reporter Jamie Joseph, "and it gives me heart-break."

Jamie Joseph, who studied solving poverty to save elephants, spoke to their class of gaunt men in tattered clothes. "There are people all over the world that think you are getting rich from killing elephants. They do not understand that you and your families drink contaminated water and go to bed hungry. Chinese criminal syndicates are stealing from Africa, from your families, and it must stop."

Rhinos—Saving the Survivors

My favorite video of a baby rhino is on Animal Planet's "Untamed, Uncut" of a calf who protected his mom. They were on the bank of a watering hole when a massive male charged, horning his mother who retreated into the water, stumbled, and slipped onto her side. The male reared his head back and rushed into the spray. Just before he stabbed her chest, her tiny baby charged his rear. Surprised, the raging male spun around to confront his puny opponent. The calf gave his mom time to get to her feet. The confused male, weighing about three tons in his huge prehistoric suit of armor, fled with the tiny baby in chase.

The courage of this calf is so inspiring. Once a calf has lost his mother, he hemorrhages fear for what he doesn't know—who will protect, love, and teach him—and what he does know—violent men with machetes. When two mammals are placed side by side in boxes and one is given an electric shock, just by listening to suffering the second one has identical brain waves and nervous system activity. One can imagine the terror of having seen his mother hacked to death. His grief is heart-wrenching.

Gertje was found next to his poached mother on May 7, 2014. He was taken to the Hoedspruit Endangered Species Center in Pretoria, South Africa. Gertje cried all night, a sound that mixes a dolphin's call with a kitten's meow. During the day, he restlessly paced, with quick shallow breaths, anxious and forlorn. To save Gertje, they found a surrogate mom, Skaap, a sheep who soothed his fear. When he was older, he was introduced to Matimba, whose mother was killed during his first mud bath. Gertje at first ran away from the miniature replica of himself, but now their bond provides vital companionship and solace in their misery.

A motorist, William Burrough, helped an eight-week-old rhino who was weak, exhausted, dehydrated, and covered in wounds. The calf lost his mother to poachers in Kruger National Park and was desperate to find a parent-shaped object. She collapsed in the shade of his car. "The tragic irony," says Burrough, "is that the calf approaches the very creatures who are responsible for her being orphaned in search of comfort. We need to let these lower forms of human life know we will not stand for senseless slaughter of our wildlife…It is our responsibility as humans

to protect these animals." Burrough called rangers. He cooled the calf down with water, and provided comfort and safety. South Africa, which has 88 percent of the remaining rhinos, shares a porous border with Mozambique, devoid of rhinos, where many poachers originate.

 After poachers killed his mother, two-month-old Donnie tried to adopt cars in Kruger National Park. His cylindrical sleekness trailed behind, then rubbed against them when they stopped. He snuggled up to a gray jeep hoping it would become his mother. Instead, he was tranquilized and put on a plane where he had a reaction to the drug and went into cardiac arrest. Amazingly, he was resuscitated and brought to a sanctuary. He will eventually be released back into the wild after he learns survival skills without his mother and overcomes his terrible grief.

Another rhino calf, Shongi, was shot in the head by poachers. Fortunately she was rescued by a veterinarian surgeon, Kobus Raath. He nurtured her back to health and provides some of what her mother would. During a mud bath, he tenderly covers her with wet clay. Then he takes off running, so she scampers up and gaily follows. She probably still misses her mother but seems to know she is loved.

Four baby rhinos—Kitui, Kiliki, Hope, and Nicky—are being raised by staff at Lewa Wildlife Conservancy in Kenya where they have ramped up efforts to protect rhinos, and lost no rhinos in 2014. There are forty-two rangers in the field who monitor the escalating poaching. Nicky has cataracts and is blind. She lives in Mike Watson's boma with her pal, a yellow labrador retriever.

Mike, Lewa's CEO, is raising funds for an eye surgeon to repair her vision.

Under a tree near the Lewa Conservancy, I visited Kitui, a Black rhino, with his twenty-four-hour armed guards. He and his brother, Kiliki, are protected by Lewa. He is the youngest of four calves of Mawingu, a blind rhino whose other offspring were killed by predators. He was shy, nudged against his guards, but approached close enough to have his upright ears and soft brown skin stroked. He's like a huge, chunky puppy with long eyelashes, knobby knees, and a triangular, puckered mouth. Nearby two massive adults, clad in body armor, crowned by magnificent horns, slept in mud. Their ancient beauty seemed prehistoric.

Poachers use silent darts to put rhinos to sleep, because they do not alert rangers. Also shooting accurately, the way one must with a rifle, isn't necessary. Anywhere you hit makes him fall immobile. Many more rhinos are being found still alive with their faces chopped up. Their suffering is horrific.

Doctors use cutting-edge technology to repair some of the damage from a machete. In South Africa, on May 18, 2015, a group of veterinarians operated on a rare survivor of poaching. The butchers chopped out the front horn but stopped partway through the back one. The four-year-old female rhino, Hope, had a 20-inch by 11-inch machete wound in her face, fracturing and damaging her nasal bone and sinus. Doctors from Saving the Survivors were fearful mud would enter her nasal cavity. They fastened many hard shields with screws over the gouge because she rubbed them loose. On August 15, they attached elephant skin, a more flexible and natural material. They hoped she'd adjust to it, but she still rubbed it off.

Photographer David Yarrow, who witnessed one operation, said the severity of her wounds were so surreal, it seemed remarkable she was alive. He imagined the elite diners in Hanoi where part of her face would be snorted and wondered if images of Hope would make them feel ashamed.

In 2012, Dr. William Fowlds found Thandi, a female, and Themba, a male, alive after their horns were hacked off. Themba fought for twenty-four days to live. He went to the watering hole to drink, slipped in, and drowned. Upon his death, Dr. Fowlds broke down in tears. "I feel so broken. Use the story of Thandi and Themba to tell the world what these animals are going through."

Thandi had pioneering skin grafts and recovered to give birth to a female calf, Thembi at the Kariega Game Reserve, on January 13, 2015. Doctors are calling the calf, all ears and knobby knees attached to a tank body, a miracle, after what happened to Thandi. Eight other survivors of horn hackings have been operated on and survived. It's heartbreaking to see the suffering caused by superstitions and fantasy cures.

From Break-up to Link-up

Albert Einstein said that our task is to widen "our circle of compassion to embrace all living creatures and the whole of nature." When we limit self-absorption, we notice landscapes are not passive backdrops. Trees are alive. They provided medicines, shelter, and food for our ancestors. Their photosynthesis emits oxygen and helps fight climate change and global warming. The trees and rivers are homes to a woodpecker hacking a tree, a moose holding his head high as he swims to shore, a beaver carving wood for a dam, a spider stepping out on his web, a sparrow's oratory of song.

In the United States, two-thirds of the land deforested, boxed, and ploughed into grids is beginning to be rewilded. In the eastern part of the country, as farms have retreated, fences are being removed and trees planted. Moose, lynx, bear, and deer are returning to their former territories. We have the resources to treat animals more generously than we do. Highways are dangerous barriers for elephants and other wildlife. In 2010, an elephant underpass was constructed under a traffic-snarled freeway in Kenya, connecting the towns of Meru and Nanyuki. By using the tall corridor, isolated herds reunite and avoid conflicts with villagers, whose crops they eat when passing by farms.

Wildlife-crossing structures help animals around human-made barriers such as roads, railroads, canals, pipelines, and power lines. Bridges protect mountain goats in Montana, Bighorn sheep in Colorado, desert tortoises in California, and panthers in Florida. In Baniff National Park, in Alberta, Canada, bridges covered with vegetation enable animals to cross over the TransCanada Highway. Gradually, communities are building structures that consider the needs of other creatures. Human civilization is inhospitable to animals. It is our job to protect them from manmade dangers.

MURDER OF CECIL BECOMES OUTRAGE TSUNAMI

In July 2015, Cecil the lion's murder began an international media roar. His beheading began a sudden, collective awakening. How could killer Walter Palmer enjoy causing suffering and death? Why would anyone show off their malicious behavior by hanging the severed head on a wall? As Nicky Campbell said, "This isn't about one lion. It is about humanity. What we are. What we value. Where we are going."

Walter Palmer is a personification of the worst in human nature. He turns life into blood, guts, and gore, and flaunts it on social media. The response is "vomitous," as late-night talk show host Jimmy Kimmel so aptly said. Palmer's cruelty created an outrage tsunami fueled by compassion for Cecil.

Jimmy Kimmel choked up when he described what Walter Palmer did to Cecil. He asks Palmer, "How was that fun? Is it that difficult for you to get an erection that you have to kill things? They have pills for that. Take one and stay home. Save yourself from being the most hated person in America." On July 29, 2015, in Bloomington, Minnesota, hundreds of protesters gathered outside Palmer's dental office. Signs read: "Palmer, there's a deep cavity waiting for you," "Rot in Hell," "The

Butcher of Bloomington." Stuffed lions were left outside the door, and in the parking lot, artist Mark Balma painted a huge portrait of Cecil as a silent protest. Many children, whose parents taught them to stand up for the voiceless, were among the crowd. Sarah Madison brought her two children. Her son wore a lion costume and carried a sign that read, "Protect me. Don't kill me." But the dentist did not have the courage to face his three-year-old critic. He temporarily closed his office.

Paula Kahumbu, of Wildlife Direct, says Palmer sounds like a psychopath who had an added thrill of wounding so many people who loved Cecil. A petition demanding justice for Cecil has over a million signatures. The White House is reviewing another petition, with over 100,000 signatures, to extradite Palmer to stand trial for his crimes. Delta Airlines, the last holdout of major US airlines, immediately stopped transport of animal trophies. Petitions to end trophy hunting circulated the Internet. On August 11, 2015, New York proposed Cecil's Law, which calls for a statewide ban on the importation, possession, and sale of big-game trophies. Jane Goodale, animal rights activist, said the happiness trophy hunters get from killing is "the joy of a diseased mind."

Comedian Bill Maher described the moral crisis in America as worshipping the filthy rich. They pay to destroy the last bits of beauty in the world by changing the laws—whatever they want to do becomes legal. Maher showed the gloat pictures of Donald Trump Jr. posing with carcasses of endangered species. "Everyone knows Donald Trump Jr. is filthy rich, but a dentist? He scrapes the tartar off people's teeth. His photos are a way of saying, 'Hey, look at me. I'm a soulless prick. I get to do something stupid and horrible only rich people can get away with.'"

Since American consumers frequently enable trophy hunters to pay huge fees, protesters hope to cut off their funds. One keyboard commenter suggested that anyone who spends money at Walter Palmer's dental office is supporting the suffering and beheading of animals. "Do not see a bloodthirsty psychopath for dental work. He may decide to add your head to his mounted collection." A cartoon on Facebook pictured an adult lion with his cub watching the horizon. "What is that orange glow, Father?" the son asks.

"That's Walter Palmer's dental surgery business on fire."

Photographer Brent Stirton published a photograph in the *Best of July 2015, National Geographic* of lion cubs on a breeding farm, ready to be sold for legalized slaughters by trophy hunters. He worries that after we have seized all their land and killed all their natural prey, lions of the future will just be manufactured commodity for trophy hunters. Without protecting their habitats, they will become extinct.

I hope we can poke a hole in our self-absorption long enough to save lions from the fate of cows, who are a human commodity with hide for shoes and flesh for steaks. Brits who volunteer to help orphaned cubs are duped into working at the breeding camps. The cubs are orphans because their parents were shot in a canned hunt. Afterward they are petted by tourists then pimped out to trophy hunters. After a life of suffering and neglect, they are disposed of and their bones are harvested for the Chinese medicine trade.

Perhaps Cecil as a symbol of animal cruelty has highlighted their fate and the free-fall in lion populations. Fifty years ago, there were 450,000 lions. Now there are only 23,000. We built, planted, and fenced away their ranges. Prides have fierce battles over lands. Most cubs die of starvation or are killed by younger males in a takeover. Trophy hunters killed 650 lions last year with horrific genetic consequences.

The strongest males, with long flowing manes, are shot. According to Dereck Joubert, the death of one male leads to twenty-three lion deaths. When nomadic males take over the territory, all the offspring are killed, as well as their mothers when they fight to defend their cubs. Lions cannot sustain the losses from trophy "hunters."

The sadistic murder of a beloved lion was a tipping point—that magic moment when an evolving issue crosses a threshold and gains significant momentum. Cecil's beheading focuses attention on the atrocities suffered by all animals, including elephants. Ivory is a trophy for Asians, showing off their wealth.

We are beginning to see that the destruction of other species by the human animal is a sign of our arrogance. "Suffering is suffering, regardless of the type of living being experiencing it," says Janice Wolf. "We are all connected on this planet and any pain, cruelty, and unkindness makes the world a colder, harsher place for all of us." War comes from feeling separate. The aggressive power of domination belongs to the Walter Palmers of the world. Trying to show you are superior by causing suffering and death is a sick game. The condemnation of Cecil's murder shows we are better than that.

"It is said that when you teach a child
to be kind to a mouse,
you do as much for the child
as you do for the mouse."

- Puja Mahajan

CONSCIOUSNESS CHANGE

Our medical marvels have tripled our lifespan. In 1920, in the United States, people lived to about fifty-two years of age. After sulfa drugs, antibiotics, and preservatives, our lifespan jumped to seventy-five. We can survive in polar regions, underwater, and in space. We can repair the body, travel to the moon, and surf cyberspace.

We are clever, but we are blinded by our brilliance. Sometimes our greatest gifts are our worst faults. Aggressive manipulation of nature has disrupted balances and depleted resources. We exploit the Earth, polluting the air, Earth, and oceans. As our technologies alter the planet, we see how vulnerable the Earth is.

As Einstein said, "No problem can be solved by the same consciousness that created it." We are raised in a cult of superiority and view other creatures as our underlings. Viewing their lives as less important than ours has led to horrific injustices. As Henry Beston says, "We patronize them for their incompleteness, for their tragic fate of having taken form so far below ourselves. And therein we err, and greatly err. For the animal shall not be measured by man. In a world older and more complete, gifted with extensions of the senses we have lost or never attained, living by voices we shall never hear. They are not brethren, they are not underlings: they are nations, caught with ourselves in the net of life and time, fellow prisoners of the splendour and travail of the earth."

Empathy for other creatures helps curb all violence. In Gujarat, India, students get a daily lesson of compassion for animals in their "Share the World" program. "It is said that when you teach a child to be kind to a mouse, you do as much for the child as you do for the mouse," says education coordinator Puja Mahajan. Children naturally have concern for animals but learn cruelty by society. There is well-documented evidence that violence toward animals is an early warning sign of violence toward humans. Officials hope their program will stem violence at large. This program, combined with an appreciation of animal wisdom, would be a way for schools to counteract violence in America.

In many ways animals, especially elephants, are more sophisticated than us. Seeing them as subordinate, we fence off, dam up, and destroy their homes and food. As the dominant life on the planet, we need to be a steward for all species, not just humans. It is time to step up to our guardianship.

In the past, laws made by humans, for humans, reflect our cultures' insensitivity to the needs of other species. The FBI has recently made animal cruelty a top-tier felony to track offenders who are prone to also hurt people. Jeff Dahmer impaled dogs, frogs, and cats on sticks. Albert DeSalvo, the Boston Strangler, trapped cats and dogs in crates and shot them. David Berkowitz, Son of Sam, poisoned his mother's parakeet. California has introduced the first law to treat animal abusers like child abusers. Those convicted would be on a registry so that neighbors might be able to protect their pets from being tortured and killed. Tracking children who hurt animals, an early sign of psychopathology, may enable them to get counseling help.

Laws are beginning to prevent the exploitation of animals and give voice to the voiceless. In the United States, there's tremendous action from grass roots organizations to ban trophy hunting as Costa Rica did.

Previously, animals were viewed as property. In August of 2015, the Oregon Supreme Court passed a landmark ruling so animals can be seen as "victims" of abuse. In May 2015, New Zealand passed a law stating that animals are "sentient beings," not "things" or "objects" but living creatures. A bill in the Canadian province of Quebec changes animals from "property" to "sentient beings." The laws add more weight to penalties in legal cases of abuse or neglect. As Peter Singer says, "All the arguments to prove man's superiority cannot shatter this hard fact: in suffering the animals are our equals."

There are desperate attempts to save rhinos from poachers. In June of 2015, ten Black rhinos were sent from Zimbabwe to Botswana where the military defends against poachers with a "shoot to kill" policy. Botswana has less corruption and a smaller human population with fewer conflicts over land. Rhinos without Borders, under the direction of filmmakers Dereck and Beverly Joubert, is airlifting one hundred rhinos from South Africa to Botswana. Another plan, still in the early stages, Rhino Drop, is to send a limited number to rural Australia.

Currently, protection of our global heritage falls on the shoulders of countries that can least afford it. If we got our priorities straight, the World Bank and the United Nations could easily afford infrastructure to erect wildlife-proof fencing to protect people from lions and elephants and to protect them from poachers or whatever else would save the Earth's treasures.

As long as we value objects over life, wildlife and wild places are in danger. European immigrants viewed America as a treasure house of goods to ransack. The insatiable desire for gold led to the massacre of Native Americans. "Gold fever" polluted the rivers with toxic chemicals. Rampant materialism had some justification then since it was a time of great poverty. Our appetite for acquisitiveness is no longer driven by hardship. We stockpile things we don't need to shore up a sense safety and self-worth.

Studies prove there is no correlation between wealth and happiness. Once our basic needs are met, our level of income does not increase happiness. External things distract us from our inner discontent, but once the thrill of the new object is over, we are on a search for more objects. Comedian Bill Maher suggests that worshipping the rich contributes to trophy hunting, a culture of crass materialism and self-aggrandizement.

In my work as a psychologist, when one person in a family develops terrible psychiatric symptoms, it says something about the family as a whole. What do Walter Palmer, Jimmy John Liautaud, and Donald Trump, Jr. say about American values? They come from successful families and are at the top of the food chain. Yet they are so cut off by arrogance, they destroy the preciousness of life for a thrill.

They illuminate the worst part of our collective soul. In our frantic race for progress, we ignore the rights of other species. Our feelings of superiority cut us off from our deepest source of sustenance. Connectedness gives us mercy, compassion, and wisdom. We need to break through our self-absorption to protect the natural world.

We need to idolize peacemakers, healers, and restorers. Indigenous cultures viewed themselves as part of the web of life. Every species had an important part. They valued wise men and shamans.

They inhabited a community of non-human presences. Each rose, each sparrow, each owl was in vibrant dialogue with the beings around it. People spoke to them, tried to understand their perspectives, and listened to them for guidance. They knew that their flesh and the flesh of the Earth were in constant dialogue.

Nature has always been our steadfast backdrop. Our environment can no longer absorb the human lust for power. The lives in balance are not just those we push to catastrophic extinction but our own. Our own survival depends on us choosing the power of love over the love of power. As Romain Gary said to elephants, "Your disappearance will mean the beginning of an entirely manmade world. But let me tell you this, old friend: in an entirely manmade world, there can be no room for man either. We are not and could never be our own creation…your presence among us carries a resonance that cannot be accounted for in terms of science or reason, but only in terms of awe, wonder, and reverence. You are our lost innocence."

HOW YOU CAN MAKE A DIFFERENCE

It may seem hard to stop the massacre of elephants by militarized terrorists a world away. But we can consider our brother and sister species as we buy things, travel and interact with animals around our neighborhood.

1. **Never buy or display ivory** – it is a symbol of death and babies left to die.
2. **Contribute to charities:**
   African Wildlife Foundation, www.awf.org
   Save the Elephants, www.savetheelephants.org
   Big Life Foundation, www.biglife.org
   Amboseli Trust for Elephants, www.amboselielephants.wildlifedirect.org
   Elephants Without Borders, www.elephantswithoutborders.org
   David Sheldrick Wildlife Trust, www.sheldrickwildlifetrust.org
3. **Give children gifts of adopting an orphan animal**. Pick an orphanage or wildlife service that will send updates and pictures so your child can get involved. As they know in Gujaret, India, teaching children compassion for animals is the first step in halting violence.
4. **Advocate for Animals.** Our laws are made by humans, for humans, and frequently ignore the rights of other species. Just because something is legal doesn't make it ethical. Advocate for the right to life of all creatures.
5. **Be compassionate about captive animals.** Some lead lives of indentured servitude – boycott circuses and elephants rides. Babies are tortured to train them to carry loads on their fragile spines. Elephants in zoos should be held in spacious enclosures with companions.
6. **Make it Safe for Wildlife.** Many people are killed when they hit deer and moose on the roads. Advocate for wildlife crossings over highways so animals can find food, water, and companions.
7. **Don't buy violent games for kids.** Many kids who slaughtered classmates spent their free time blowing up fantasy people. Then, when angry and mentally ill, they blew up real people.
8. **Teach your kids to value life over objects**. Get them out of the virtual world to marvel at the real world – caterpillars, rabbits, owls all have purpose, magic and beauty.

The keepers of baby elephants, who mend our innocent gardeners of the earth, seem to resonate with poet Mary Oliver. "I love this world even its hard places," she thought, as she fumbled a broken gull from the sand into a box and "toward a place where sometimes things can be mended.....Even if the effort comes to nothing, you have to do something....I keep my eyes on the road... as the gull beats the air with its good wing." To love this world, she says, we must hold what is mortal against our bones, as if the whole world depends on it.

We all are imperfect in a broken world. But we can make a difference by becoming angels of mercy. Beating the air with our good wing, we can help the hurt, the injured, and the helpless newborns. *Save the world's broken trumpets. Do not go quietly into the night of extinction.*

Oliver says that there are a hundred paths through the world easier than love, but who wants easier? Our own survival depends on us choosing the power of love over the love of power.

Senator Jason Lewis, co-author of the bill to halt ivory trade in MA, Cynthia Mead and John Linehan of Zoo New England, Dr. Amy Shroff, and Tom Lang march against extinction.

CPSIA information can be obtained
at www.ICGtesting.com
Printed in the USA
BVOW05s0858181116
468211BV00024B/165/P